DEFENSE, SECURITY AND STRATEGIES

DIRTY MONEY

CROSS-BORDER MONEY LAUNDERING

DEFENSE, SECURITY AND STRATEGIES

Additional books in this series can be found on Nova's website under the Series tab.

Additional E-books in this series can be found on Nova's website under the E-book tab.

DEFENSE, SECURITY AND STRATEGIES

DIRTY MONEY

CROSS-BORDER MONEY LAUNDERING

DONNA P. RICHARDS
EDITOR

Nova Science Publishers, Inc.
New York

For permission to use material from this book please contact us:
Telephone 631-231-7269; Fax 631-231-8175
Web Site: http://www.novapublishers.com

Library of Congress Cataloging-in-Publication Data

Dirty money : cross-border money laundering / editors, Donna P. Richards.
p. cm.
Includes reprints of legislative branch materials.
Includes bibliographical references and index.
ISBN 978-1-61324-663-4 (hardcover : alk. paper) 1. Transnational crime--United States. 2. Money laundering--United States. 3. Drug traffic--United States. 4. Border security--United States. I. Richards, Donna P. II. United States. Congress. Senate. Caucus on International Narcotics Control
HV6252.5.U6D57 2011
364.16'8--dc22
2011015366

Published by Nova Science Publishers, Inc. † New York

CONTENTS

PREFACE

This book examines U.S. efforts to stem cross-border money laundering through the use of devices called stored value, such as prepaid cards and the corresponding regulatory gaps that may exist.

Chapter 1- U.S. Customs and Border Protection (CBP) is the lead federal agency responsible for inspecting travelers who seek to smuggle large volumes of cash—called bulk cash—when leaving the country through land ports of entry. It is estimated that criminals smuggle $18 billion to $39 billion a year in bulk cash across the southwest border. The Financial Crimes Enforcement Network (FinCEN) is responsible for reducing the risk of cross-border smuggling of funds through the use of devices called stored value, such as prepaid cards. GAO was asked to examine (1) the extent of actions taken by CBP to stem the flow of bulk cash leaving the country and any challenges that remain, (2) the regulatory gaps, if any, of cross-border reporting and other anti-money laundering requirements of stored value, and (3) if gaps exist, the extent to which FinCEN has addressed them. To conduct its work, GAO observed outbound operations at five land ports of entry. GAO also reviewed statutes, rules, and other information for stored value. This is a public version of a law enforcement sensitive report that GAO issued in September 2010. Information CBP deemed sensitive has been redacted.

Chapter 2- Hearing on Money Laundering and Bulk Cash Smuggling across the Southwest Border held by the Senate Caucus on International Narcotics Control on March 9, 2011.

Chapter 3- Statement of Richard M. Stana before the Senate Caucus on International Narcotics Control on March 9, 2011 regarding Moving Illegal Proceeds.

Chapter 4- Testimony of Alan Bersin before the Senate Caucus on International Narcotics Control on March 9, 2011 regarding Money Laundering and Bulk Cash Smuggling along the Southwest Border.

Chapter 5 – Statement of Kumar C. Kibble before the Senate Caucus on International Narcotics Control on March 9, 2011 regarding regarding Money Laundering and Bulk Cash Smuggling along the Southwest Border.

Chapter 6 – Statement of Jamal El-Hindi before the Senate Caucus on International Narcotics Control on March 9, 2011 regarding Money Laundering and Bulk Cash Smuggling along the Southwest Border.

Chapter 7- Money laundering is a federal crime, most often prosecuted today under 18 U.S.C. 1956. Money laundering is commonly understood as the process of cleansing the taint from the proceeds of crime. In federal criminal law, it is more. In varying degrees under federal law, money laundering involves the flow of resources to and from several hundred other federal, state and foreign crimes. It consists of: (1) engaging in a financial transaction involving the proceeds of certain crimes in order to conceal the nature, source, or ownership of proceeds they produced; (2) transporting funds generated by certain criminal activities internationally in order to promote further criminal activities, or to conceal nature, source, or ownership of the criminal proceeds, or to evade reporting requirements; (3) engaging in a financial transaction involving the proceeds of certain crimes in order to promote further offenses; (4) engaging in a financial transaction involving criminal proceeds in order to evade taxes on the income produced by the illicit activity; (5) structuring financial transactions in order to evade reporting requirements; (6) spending more than $10,000 of the proceeds of certain criminal activities; (7) traveling in interstate or foreign commerce in order to distribute the proceeds of certain criminal activities; (8) transmitting the proceeds of criminal activity in the course of a money transmitting business; (9) smuggling unreported cash across a U.S. border, or (10) failing to comply with the Treasury Department's anti-money laundering provisions. The Supreme Court has recently indicated that the proscription in section 1956 against attempted international transportation of tainted proceeds to conceal their source, ownership, nature or ultimate location does not reach simple attempted cash smuggling without some proof of a specific concealment purpose for the smuggling. It indicated in a second case that references to the tainted "proceeds," which are the focus of section 1956, sometimes refer to the profits of a predicate offense and sometimes to its gross receipts.

In: Dirty Money
Editor: Donna P. Richards

ISBN: 978-1-61324-663-4

Chapter 1

CHALLENGES EXIST IN THE FEDERAL GOVERNMENT'S EFFORT TO STEM CROSS-BORDER CURRENCY SMUGGLING

United States Government Accountability Office

WHY GAO DID THIS STUDY

U.S. Customs and Border Protection (CBP) is the lead federal agency responsible for inspecting travelers who seek to smuggle large volumes of cash—called bulk cash—when leaving the country through land ports of entry. It is estimated that criminals smuggle $18 billion to $39 billion a year in bulk cash across the southwest border. The Financial Crimes Enforcement Network (FinCEN) is responsible for reducing the risk of cross-border smuggling of funds through the use of devices called stored value, such as prepaid cards. GAO was asked to examine (1) the extent of actions taken by CBP to stem the flow of bulk cash leaving the country and any challenges that remain, (2) the regulatory gaps, if any, of cross-border reporting and other anti-money laundering requirements of stored value, and (3) if gaps exist, the extent to which FinCEN has addressed them. To conduct its work, GAO observed outbound operations at five land ports of entry. GAO also reviewed statutes, rules, and other information for stored value. This is a public version of a law enforcement sensitive report that GAO issued in September 2010. Information CBP deemed sensitive has been redacted.

What GAO Recommends

GAO recommends that CBP, among other things, gather data on program costs and benefits and that FinCEN develop a plan, including target dates, to better manage its rulemaking process. CBP and FinCEN concurred with these recommendations.

What GAO Found

In March 2009, CBP created an Outbound Enforcement Program aimed at stemming the flow of bulk cash leaving the country, but further actions could be taken to address program challenges. Under the program, CBP inspects travelers leaving the country at all 25 land ports of entry along the southwest border. On the Northern border, inspections are conducted at the discretion of the Port Director. From March 2009 through June 2010, CBP seized about $41 million in illicit bulk cash leaving the country at land ports of entry. Stemming the flow of bulk cash, however, is a difficult and challenging task. For example, CBP is unable to inspect every traveler leaving the country at land ports of entry and smugglers of illicit goods have opportunities to circumvent the inspection process. Other challenges involve limited technology, infrastructure, and procedures to support outbound operations. CBP is in the early phases of this program and has not yet taken some actions to gain a better understanding of how well the program is working, such as gathering data for measuring program costs and benefits. By gathering data for measuring expected program costs and benefits, CBP could be in a better position to weigh the costs of any proposed expansion of the outbound inspection program against likely outcomes.

Regulatory gaps of cross-border reporting and other anti-money laundering requirements exist with the use of stored value. For example, travelers must report transporting more than $10,000 in monetary instruments or currency at one time when leaving the country, but FinCEN does not have a similar requirement for travelers transporting stored value. Similarly, certain anti- money laundering regulations, such as reports on suspicious activities, do not apply to the entire stored value industry. The nature and extent of the use of stored value for cross-border currency smuggling and other illegal activities remains unknown, but federal law enforcement agencies are concerned about its use.

FinCEN is developing regulations, as required by the Credit CARD Act of 2009, to address gaps in regulations related to the use of stored value for criminal purposes, but much work remains. FinCEN has not developed a management plan that includes, among other things, target dates for completing the regulations. Developing such a plan could help FinCEN better manage its rulemaking effort. When it issues the regulations, law enforcement agencies and FinCEN may be challenged in ensuring compliance by travelers and industry. For example, FinCEN will be responsible for numerous tasks including issuing guidance for compliance examiners, revising the way in which it tracks suspicious activities related to stored value, and addressing gaps in anti-money laundering regulations for off-shore entities that issue and sell stored value.

ABBREVIATIONS

APA	Administration Procedure Act
BEST	Border Enforcement Security Task Force
BSA	Bank Secrecy Act
CBP	Customs and Border Protection
CMIR	Report of International Transportation of Currency or Monetary Instrument
CTR	Currency transaction report
DEA	Drug Enforcement Administration
DHS	Department of Homeland Security
DOJ	Department of Justice
EPIC	El Paso Intelligence Center
FATF	Financial Crimes Enforcement Network
FBI	Federal Bureau of Investigation
FinCEN	Financial Crimes Enforcement Network
IRS	Internal Revenue Service
MSB	Money services business
NBFI	Nonbank financial institution
NDIC	National Drug Intelligence Center
NPRM	Notice of Proposed Rulemaking
OFO	Office of Field Operations
OMB	Office of Management and Budget
SAR	Suspicious activity report
SB/SE	Small Business/Self Employed Division

Treasury Department of the Treasury

October 25, 2010

The Honorable Max Baucus
Chairman
Committee on Finance
United States Senate

The Honorable Jeff Bingaman
United States Senate

Moving illegal proceeds across our nation's borders presents a significant threat to national security. Mexican drug trafficking organizations, terrorist organizations, and other groups with malevolent intent finance their operations by moving funds into or out of the United States. For example, a common technique used for taking proceeds from drug sales in the United States to Mexico is a method known as bulk cash smuggling.[1] Smuggling methods can involve taking bulk cash by private or commercial vehicles through land ports of entry, by private plane or boat through air and sea ports of entry, or through other means, including underground tunnels, parcels sent by mail, or by foot between ports of entry. Because of its clandestine nature, the extent of bulk cash smuggling is difficult to quantify with any certainty. The National Drug Intelligence Center (NDIC) estimates that proceeds from drug trafficking generated in this country are smuggled across the southwest border and the proceeds total between $18 billion and $39 billion a year.[2] NDIC also estimates that Canadian drug trafficking organizations smuggle significant amounts of cash across the Northern border from proceeds of drugs sold in the United States. In the largest known case of bulk cash smuggling, over two tons of currency, mostly in $100 banknotes, totaling $205 million was seized in Mexico City in 2007. In addition to bulk cash smuggling, 21st century methods and technologies of laundering money have emerged. In 2009, the NDIC stated that new financial products and technologies present unique opportunities for money launderers as well as unprecedented challenges to the intelligence, law enforcement, and regulatory communities.[3] Among other money laundering techniques, NDIC and others cited the use of prepaid cards or gift cards that are loaded with currency or value—also called stored value—as presenting a compact and easily transportable method that has been used to move money into and out of the United States.[4] U.S. law enforcement officials agree that stored value is an emerging cash alternative for legitimate consumers and criminals alike.[5]

U.S. Customs and Border Protection (CBP)—a major component in the Department of Homeland Security (DHS)—is the lead federal agency in charge of securing our nation's borders. CBP carries out its responsibility by, among other things, inspecting travelers at land, air, and sea ports of entry.[6] In March 2009, the Secretary of Homeland Security called on CBP to help stem the flow of bulk cash and weapons moving south by inspecting travelers leaving the United States for Mexico. As a result of this request, CBP increased its effort to stem the flow of bulk cash smuggling. This effort—called outbound operations—expanded CBP's primary mission of inspecting travelers who seek to enter the United States. In addition to addressing the threat of bulk cash and arms that leave the country, CBP outbound operations may also, among other things, identify and pursue criminals or fugitives attempting to flee the country and travelers who attempt to take stolen vehicles across the border. CBP's responsibility for inspecting travelers who leave the country is a difficult task because it must also facilitate the cross-border movement of legitimate travelers and billions of dollars in international trade.

The Financial Crimes Enforcement Network (FinCEN)—a bureau in the Department of the Treasury[7]—seeks to deter and detect criminal activity and safeguard the financial system from the risk that terrorists and other criminals may fund their operations through financial institutions in the United States. Among other things, FinCEN is responsible for administering certain laws aimed at preventing criminals from abusing financial systems in the United States.

Given the important role that CBP and FinCEN play in national security, you asked us to review the progress that they have made in stemming the flow of bulk cash leaving the country and in ensuring financial entities whose businesses involve stored value carry out anti-money laundering practices, respectively. In response, in September 2010, we issued a law enforcement sensitive report to you that addressed the following questions:

- To what extent has CBP taken actions to stem the flow of bulk cash leaving the country through land ports of entry and what challenges, if any, remain?
- What regulatory gaps, if any, exist for cross-border reporting and other anti-money laundering requirements involving the use of stored value?

- If any regulatory gaps exist for cross-border reporting and other anti-money laundering requirements involving the use of stored value, to what extent has FinCEN taken action to address them?

This report is a public version of the prior sensitive report that we provided to you. DHS deemed some of the information in the prior report as law enforcement sensitive, which must be protected from public disclosure. Therefore, this report omits sensitive information about CBP's outbound inspection efforts, including techniques used to carry out inspections and data on staffing, infrastructure, and technology that support outbound inspections. In addition, at DHS's request, we have redacted data on the specific ports of entry where bulk cash has been seized. Although the information provided in this report is more limited in scope, it addresses the same questions as the sensitive report. Also, the overall methodology used for both reports is the same.

To address the question on CBP efforts to stem the flow of bulk cash leaving the country at land ports of entry, we conducted site visits, reviewed CBP data, and interviewed CBP officials. We visited and observed outbound operations at five ports of entry (Blaine, Washington; Buffalo, New York; El Paso, Texas; Laredo, Texas; and San Ysidro, California). We selected these ports of entry to provide us with examples of outbound operations at land ports of entry on the Northern and southwest border that have high volumes of traffic. At each location, we interviewed managers and CBP officers knowledgeable about outbound operations to determine actions that have been taken to stem the flow of bulk cash as well as ways to strengthen the program. While we cannot generalize our work from our site visits to all ports of entry, the results from this work provided us with valuable insights about outbound operations. Among other things, we reviewed and analyzed data on the amount of bulk cash seized from March 2009 through June 2010. We assessed the reliability of these data by interviewing staff responsible for the data and reviewing relevant documentation. We concluded that these data were sufficiently reliable for the purposes of our review. We reviewed data on the number of license plate readers installed on outbound lanes as of July 2010. We interviewed CBP staff responsible for collecting these data and determined that the data were sufficient for our review. We also reviewed CBP's policies and procedures and strategic plan for its outbound operations. We interviewed staff at CBP headquarters involved in (1) implementing the outbound program and (2) assessing staffing, technology, and equipment for outbound operations. We also reviewed documents on the budget for outbound operations, policy guidance, and relevant statutes related to bulk cash smuggling. We reviewed assessments of bulk cash smuggling, including the 2009 and 2010 National Drug Threat Assessments issued by the National Drug Intelligence Center,[8] a National Drug Intelligence Center report on bulk cash smuggling,[9] and a Mexican Bulk Currency study issued by U.S. Immigration and Customs Enforcement (ICE).[10] We found these assessments to be acceptable for use in our report. We also reviewed January 2010 data from the Texas Center for Border Economic and Enterprise Development and interviewed center staff members to determine the reliability of the data. We concluded that the data were sufficiently reliable for our review. In addition, our investigators tested outbound operations at three ports of entry on the southwest border. Our investigators did their work in accordance with quality standards for investigations established by the Council of the Inspectors General on Quality and Efficiency. While we cannot generalize the work of our investigators to all ports of entry, the results from this work provided us with valuable insights about outbound operations. We reviewed *Standards for Internal Control in the Federal Government* and compared the standards for monitoring and controls with CBP's policies and procedures and performance measures for its Outbound Enforcement Program.[11] Our scope did not include an examination of outbound operations at air or sea ports of entry.

To address the questions on regulatory gaps, if any, of cross-border reporting and anti-money laundering requirements involving the use of stored value and the status of FinCEN efforts to address any identified gaps, we reviewed and analyzed information on the ways in which stored value has been used to smuggle currency across the nation's borders and to launder money. We also reviewed current regulations and statutes that govern issuers, sellers, and redeemers of stored value. To obtain further information on vulnerabilities related to stored value, we interviewed officials or obtained information from federal law enforcement agencies that are involved in efforts to interdict or investigate the illicit use of stored value, including ICE, the U.S. Secret Service, and CBP— components in DHS, the Federal Bureau of Investigation (FBI) and the Drug Enforcement Administration (DEA)— components in the Department of Justice (DOJ), and Criminal Investigation of the Internal Revenue Service (IRS)—a component in the Department of the Treasury (Treasury). In addition, we reviewed a random, probability sample of 400 reports on suspicious activities submitted by depository institutions and money services businesses (MSB) from October 2008 through April 2010 to identify examples of suspicious activities related to stored value.[12,13] To obtain information on the status of Treasury's efforts to address identified vulnerabilities (on stored value), we interviewed officials from Treasury's Office of Terrorism and Financial Intelligence, FinCEN, and the Office of Fraud/Bank Secrecy Act, within IRS' Small Business/Self Employed Division (SB/SE). We reviewed relevant legislation, such as the Credit Card Accountability Responsibility and Disclosure Act of 2009 (Credit CARD Act)[14] and the Notice of Proposed Rulemaking related to stored value issued by Treasury in June 2010.[15] We also reviewed OMB's guidelines and requirements for the rulemaking process. Finally, we reviewed *Standards for Internal Control in the Federal Government*[16] and compared the standards for monitoring with FinCEN's policies and procedures for monitoring MSBs.

We conducted this performance audit from June 2009 through September 2010 in accordance with generally accepted government auditing standards. Those standards require that we plan and perform the audit to obtain sufficient, appropriate evidence to provide a reasonable basis for our findings and conclusions based on our audit objectives. We believe that the evidence obtained provides a reasonable basis for our findings and conclusions based on our audit objectives.

BACKGROUND

CBP Is the Lead Federal Agency Responsible for Stemming the Flow of Bulk Cash Leaving the U.S. at Land Ports of Entry

CBP is the lead federal agency charged with securing our nation's borders while facilitating legitimate travel and commerce.[17] To meet the Secretary's March 2009 mandate that CBP conduct inspections of traffic leaving the U.S. for Mexico at all 25 land ports of entry on the southwest border, CBP expanded or initiated inspections of outbound travelers, including those leaving by foot, private vehicle (see figure 1), or commercial trucks. CBP's effort to stem the flow of bulk cash is part of a larger counternarcotics strategy to secure the southwest border.[18]

CBP has three main components that have border security responsibilities. First, CBP's Office of Field Operations is responsible for inspecting the flow of people and goods that enter and leave the country through air, land, and sea ports of entry. Second, CBP's Border Patrol works to prevent the illegal entry of persons and merchandise, including contraband, into and out of the United States between the ports of entry and at checkpoints located in major traffic routes away from the border. In doing so, the Border Patrol is responsible for controlling nearly 7,000 miles of the nation's land borders between ports of entry and 95,000 miles of maritime border in partnership with the United States Coast Guard. Third, CBP's Office of Air and Marine helps to protect the nation's people and critical infrastructure through the coordinated use of an integrated force of air and marine resources and provides mission support to the other CBP components. For fiscal year 2010, CBP had a $11.4 billion budget, of which $2.7 billion was for border security and trade facilitation at ports of entry. For outbound operations, CBP's budget was about $109 million in fiscal year 2009 and is an estimated $145 million for fiscal year 2010.

In carrying out its responsibilities, CBP operates 327 ports of entry, composed of airports, seaports, and designated land ports of entry along the Northern and southwest border.[19] While CBP does not know the number of travelers that leave the United States through land ports of entry, it estimates that it inspected over 360 million travelers who entered the country in fiscal year 2009 through land, air, and sea ports of entry. In total, the number of travelers who entered the country through land ports of entry represented over 70 percent of all travelers entering the country.

Source: GAO.

Figure 1. CBP Officers Conducting Outbound Inspections.

Source: GAO.

Figure 2. CBP Officers Querying Travelers Leaving the United States.

CBP's Process for Inspecting Travelers Leaving the Country

The process used by CBP to inspect travelers leaving the country differs from the inspection process for those entering the United States at land ports of entry. CBP centers attention, among other things, on the citizenship and admissibility of the travelers for those who seek to enter or reenter the country through land ports of entry.[20] In contrast, CBP officers ask a different set of questions of travelers leaving the country. To determine whether travelers are in compliance with the reporting requirements for the international transport of currency and monetary instruments,[21] officers may ask travelers whether they (1) intend to leave the country by asking where they are going (i.e., Mexico on the southwest border and Canada on the Northern border), (2) are carrying more than $10,000 in currency, checks, money orders, or any other type of monetary instrument,[22] and (3) are transporting any weapons or ammunition into Mexico or Canada.[23] While carrying more than $10,000 in currency or other type of monetary instrument across the border is legal, failure to report the currency or monetary instrument with the intent to evade the reporting requirement is illegal. Further, it is illegal for an individual to knowingly conceal more than $10,000 in currency or other monetary instruments and transport or attempt to transport such currency or monetary instruments into or out of the United States with the intent of evading the reporting requirements.[24] In addition to the interview process, CBP officers may also inspect, among other things, the content of car trunks, vehicle compartments, and packages in the vehicle. Figure 2 shows CBP officers querying outbound travelers at a land port of entry.

When conducting outbound operations, CBP officers may refer travelers for a more detailed inspection—called secondary inspection. Secondary inspections generally involve inspections of vehicles in a separate area from the primary inspection. They can include more in-depth interviewing of travelers, checking the traveler's identifying information against law enforcement databases, or inspecting containers and boxes (see figure 3).

FinCEN Plays a Key Role in Regulating Money Services Businesses

While smuggling cash is one method of taking illegal proceeds out of the country, criminals have also begun using other means to move proceeds from illegal activities across U.S. borders. One such method is the use of electronic media called stored value. This method can involve a broad range of technologies, including the use of prepaid cards, prepaid telephone cards, and financial transactions carried out through a cell phone.[25] Money services businesses play a key role in issuing, selling, and redeeming stored value.

Figure 3. Secondary Inspection of an Outbound Vehicle.

FinCEN, a bureau within the Department of the Treasury, is responsible for the administration of the Bank Secrecy Act (BSA)[26]—a statute that authorizes FinCEN to require MSBs and other financial institutions as well as nonfinancial trades or businesses and many individuals to maintain records and file reports that have a high degree of usefulness in criminal, tax, regulatory investigations or procedures, or certain types of counterterrorism investigations.[27] FinCEN carries out this responsibility as part of its broad mission of enhancing U.S. national security, deterring and detecting criminal activity, and safeguarding financial systems from abuse by among other things, requiring financial institutions to establish anti-money laundering programs as well as file reports on large currency transactions. [28] FinCEN has about 300 staff to carry out its analytical, administrative, and regulatory responsibilities.[29] Within FinCEN, the Regulatory Policy and Programs Division is responsible for, among other things, BSA compliance in the financial industry and for issuing regulations for U.S. financial institutions.

To carry out its mission, FinCEN supports and networks with law enforcement agencies across the federal government that may be involved in investigating money laundering and terrorism financing.[30] For example, FinCEN works with agencies in DHS, such as CBP, ICE, and Secret Service; agencies in DOJ, including the DEA, Bureau of Alcohol, Tobacco, Firearms, and Explosives, and the FBI; and the Criminal Investigation Division within the IRS. In addition, FinCEN coordinates its efforts with another IRS unit called the Small Business/Self Employed Division which conducts BSA compliance examinations of certain nonfederally regulated non-bank financial institutions, such as MSBs and casinos.

MSBs Play a Key Role in Offering Stored Value Products to Consumers

Among the businesses that FinCEN has defined as MSBs are those that issue, sell, or redeem stored value.[31] In some cases, such businesses may provide a variety of services in addition to offering stored value products, including check cashing, money orders, and money transmitting services. In other cases, such businesses may only issue, sell, or redeem stored value. These businesses play a key role in providing financial services to a segment of the population that may not maintain checking or savings accounts. Such businesses are common and are located in large and small communities across the country. Examples of MSBs can range from national companies with a large number of agents and branches, such as Western Union and MoneyGram, to small "mom and pop" money services businesses that may offer check cashing, money orders, and other financial services. The volume of transactions for MSBs nationwide is not known.[32]

One type of product offered by MSBs that falls under the definition of stored value are stored value cards, which include gift cards or prepaid cards. In this report, we will refer to such cards as stored value cards, the same term that FinCEN currently uses for such products.[33] Stored value cards are a growing alterative to cash transactions and they offer individuals without bank accounts an alternative to cash and money orders. They have many legitimate uses that help consumers in a variety of ways. For example, retail establishments sell gift cards to customers as an easy and convenient way to purchase goods or services. Employers may issue cards in lieu of checks when paying salaries to employees.

Consumers can also purchase cards and use them to purchase goods or services at retail stores across the country or to, in some cases, withdraw cash at automated teller machines overseas. For example, rather than paying for groceries using cash, a consumer could use a prepaid card. Also, the federal government uses prepaid cards in conjunction with its food stamp program.

The two main types of stored value cards are the following.

- Closed system cards (see figure 4)—These are the most common form of stored value cards and are often called gift cards. These cards are issued by major merchants and retailers, such as department stores, electronics stores, and coffee shops. They can be bought at many different types of retailers, including drugstores, grocery stores, and other businesses. Other examples include cards that students may use to purchase food on college campuses or that passengers use on subway systems or phone cards. Generally, closed system cards are limited in use in that they can only be used to purchase goods or services from a single merchant. These cards may be limited to the initial value posted to the card or may allow the card holder to add value. A study conducted for the Federal Reserve estimated that in 2006, the value of transactions for closed system cards amounted to $36.6 billion.[34]
- Open system cards—These cards have greater use as a cash alternative since a single card may be used at a myriad of stores, merchants, or automated teller machines (ATM) within and across U.S. borders. Such cards are easy to buy and can be bought on-line or

in person. Open system cards may not require a bank account or face-to-face verification of the card holder's identity. Domestically, companies may voluntarily place a dollar limit on the cards. Such cards may be used to access cash from ATMs in and out of the United States and can be reloaded to add value on the card. In certain countries outside of the United States, open system cards can be purchased and can be used to withdraw cash at ATMs across the world. A study conducted for the Federal Reserve estimated that in 2006, the value of transactions for open system cards in the United States totaled $13.2 billion.[35]

Hybrid forms of closed system and open system cards are also available. One form of a semi-closed system card can be used at more than one store rather than a single store. For example, a shopper may be able to use a card at a group of stores located in the same shopping mall. Another example of a hybrid card is one that can be used at any merchant that accepts debit or credit cards, but the card cannot be used to withdraw cash at ATMs.

Source: DOJ.

Figure 4. Examples of Closed System Stored Value Cards.

The Departments of Treasury, Justice, and Homeland Security recognized stored value as a potential threat for cross-border currency smuggling and money laundering as early as 2005.[36] For example, law enforcement agencies from these three departments stated that "stored value cards provide a compact, easily transportable, and potentially anonymous way to store and access cash value" and that "federal law enforcement agencies have reported [that such devices have been] used as alternatives to smuggling physical cash." Further, they stated that "the volume of dirty money circulating through the United States is undeniably vast and criminals are enjoying new advantages with globalization and the advent of new financial services such as stored value cards." A year later, in 2006, a Treasury official stated that while stored value cards serve legitimate markets, without adequate controls, such payment innovations pose significant risks for money laundering and terrorist financing. This official noted that the risks involved access to bank payment networks without requiring a bank account or verifying customer identification.

Beyond cards, new forms of stored value have surfaced in recent years. In 2008, the World Bank issued a report that identified the risk of international smuggling and money laundering of illegal proceeds through the use of financial transactions initiated from a mobile phone, also called mobile financial services.[37] That report describes how technology is now available in countries such as South Korea, the Philippines, and Malaysia that allows individuals to make transactions from an account in one country to an account in another country through a mobile phone. This technology has begun to penetrate the market in the United States and will become more readily available to consumers in the next several years. According to the report, the risks of money laundering with the use of such devices include (1) user identity may not be known, (2) "smurfing," or splitting large financial transactions into smaller transactions, can be carried out to evade scrutiny and reporting by the financial institution, and (3) mobile financial services fall outside of anti-money laundering regulations.

CBP HAS ESTABLISHED AN OUTBOUND ENFORCEMENT PROGRAM, BUT FURTHER ACTIONS ARE NEEDED TO ADDRESS PROGRAM CHALLENGES

CBP Has Created an Outbound Enforcement Program and Seized about $41 Million in Bulk Cash Leaving the Country Since March 2009

In March 2009, CBP reestablished an Outbound Enforcement Program within its Office of Field Operations (OFO).[38] The immediate goal of the program was to increase outbound enforcement activities along the southwest border in order to obstruct the illegal flow of firearms and currency being smuggled from the United States to the Mexican Drug Trafficking Organizations.[39] The program is staffed by a Director and 6 other officials. Since March 2009, CBP officers conducting outbound operations have conducted more than 3 million inspections.[40]

In addition to increasing outbound inspections, CBP has taken further action to support its efforts to seize bulk cash and other items. For example, CBP has developed a training curriculum that provides officer training in outbound enforcement operations for all port environments, including land, air, and sea. The training curriculum includes a 6-part, Web-based, training series, an 8-day classroom session, and on-the-job training. During the classroom session, officers complete modules on legal authority, targeting, inspecting, and processing, and participate in scenario-based activities.[41] As of July 2010, 131 officers had completed the training in fiscal year 2010.[42] In addition to developing outbound training, the Outbound Enforcement Division integrates the work of outbound operations with other CBP components. For example, the Division coordinates with the Tactical Operations Division and the Office of Intelligence and Operations Coordination to develop tactical and strategic operations based on a review of intelligence information and seizure activity. Further, the Division coordinates its efforts with staff involved in carrying out the Western Hemisphere Travel Initiative as well as with the Office of Border Patrol.[43] For example, outbound enforcement efforts are augmented by 116 Border Patrol agents.

OFO also coordinates its efforts with other law enforcement entities working to combat bulk cash smuggling, such as DEA and ICE. For example, CBP coordinates with DEA by providing staff and intelligence to the El Paso Intelligence Center (EPIC), a national tactical intelligence center led by DEA and designed to support law enforcement efforts, with a significant emphasis on the southwest border. Among other functions, EPIC analyzes bulk cash seizure data and develops various reports on bulk cash smuggling methods, which are provided to various law enforcement agencies. EPIC also responds to requests for bulk currency seizure data from officers in the field. Additionally, CBP participates with ICE in Operation Firewall and the Border Enforcement Security Task Force (BEST) initiative. Operation Firewall, started in 2005, targets criminal organizations involved in outbound currency smuggling, while the BEST initiative focuses on increasing information sharing and collaboration among agencies involved in disrupting and dismantling criminal organizations that pose a significant threat to border security.

As a result of its outbound enforcement activities, CBP seized about $41 million in illicit bulk cash leaving the country at land ports of entry from March 2009 through June 2010. The vast majority of this currency, 97 percent, was seized along the southwest border.[44] While CBP seized more than twice the amount of bulk cash during the first year of the outbound program as compared to the year prior,[45] total seizures account for a small percentage of the estimated $18 billion to $39 billion in illicit proceeds being smuggled across the southwest border and out of the United States annually.[46]

CBP was most successful in seizing bulk cash during the first 6 months of the Outbound Enforcement Program. As shown in table 1 below, CBP seized nearly $21 million from March 2009 through August 2009, averaging about $3.5 million each month. Despite the number of seizures increasing by 17 percent during the second 6 months of the outbound program, the total amount of cash seized decreased by 37 percent when compared to the first 6-month period.

The amount of cash seized in any given month varied. As shown in figure 5 below, since the start of the Outbound Enforcement Program, total seizures spiked in March, April, and September 2009. The spikes in March and April 2009, totaling $6.4 million and $8.2 million respectively, were each driven by a single incident in which CBP seized a large amount of currency. For example, of the $6.4 million CBP seized in March 2009 across all ports of entry, CBP seized more than $3 million during a single incident at a port of entry. In contrast, the $6.3 million spike in September is comprised of multiple seizures of smaller amounts of currency, with no single seizure larger than $803,000.

Table 1. Bulk Cash Seizures at Land Ports of Entry on the Northern and Southwest Border

		Preprogram seizures		Program seizures	
		Mar. 2008 – Aug. 2008	Sept. 2008 – Feb. 2009	First 6 months: Mar. 2009 – Aug. 2009	Second 6 months: Sept.2009 – Feb. 2010
Cash seized	Total	$4,731,555	$12,058,277	$20,842,679	$13,121,700
	Monthly average	$788,593	$2,009,713	$3,473,780	$2,186,950
Seizure events	Total	159	180	198	231
	Monthly average	27	30	33	39

Source: GAO analysis of BorderStat data.

From March 2009 through June 2010, CBP had at least one bulk cash seizure at 21 of the 25 land ports of entry along the southwest border while conducting outbound operations;[47] however, the total amount seized varied significantly by port. Along the southwest border, the total cash seized at each port during this time period ranged from about $11,000 to about $11 million, with more than 80 percent of the cash seized at 5 land ports. Two ports represent about half of all seizures. CBP officials stated that the concentration of seizures in these 5 land ports may be the result of high-traffic volumes and proximity to major drug trafficking routes.

In addition to bulk cash seizures, CBP's Outbound Enforcement Program has carried out other enforcement actions, such as firearm seizures, drug seizures, stolen vehicle recoveries, and enforcement of immigration violations. Examples include the following:

- In April 2010, officers conducting outbound operations at the San Ysidro port of entry in California apprehended a male subject wanted in Mexico for a triple homicide, trafficking of cocaine, methamphetamines, firearms, and ammunitions.
- In June 2010, officers conducting outbound operations at the San Luis, Arizona port of entry seized a large sports utility vehicle, 114 grenades, and over 2,500 rounds of various types of ammunition.

Stemming the Flow of Bulk Cash Is a Challenging Task

CBP has succeeded in establishing an Outbound Enforcement Program, but the program is in its early phases and there is a general recognition by CBP managers and officers that the agency's ability to stem the flow of bulk cash is limited because of the difficulty in detecting bulk cash. Beyond the inherent difficulty in identifying travelers who attempt to smuggle cash, three main factors limit CBP's success in this area.

First, CBP currently does not conduct outbound operations on a full-time basis, providing smugglers opportunities to circumvent detection by crossing the border when CBP officers are not conducting operations. Second, officers have limited equipment, technology, and infrastructure for conducting outbound operations. CBP officers and managers report that additional resources would improve officer effectiveness at discovering bulk cash and enhance officer safety. CBP began a $23 million project to determine how to deploy additional technology to outbound lanes in 2009 and expect cost estimates to be ready in September 2010. CBP also plans to spend approximately $10 million in funds from the Fiscal Year 2009 Supplemental Appropriations Act[48] for temporary infrastructure improvements and to install additional infrastructure at up to 21 crossings on the southwest border starting in February 2011. Third, long wait times impact CBP's ability to inspect all outbound travelers given CBP's need to balance its mission of facilitating the cross-border movement of legitimate travelers and billions of dollars in international trade with its mission of inspecting travelers. Additional data and information on the challenges CBP faces in stemming the flow of bulk cash smuggling is law enforcement sensitive and not included in this report.

While factors such as staffing, infrastructure, and technology limit CBP's ability to detect large amounts of cash, the fact that CBP conducts outbound inspections does not guarantee that the agency will identify attempts to smuggle bulk cash. For example, our investigators tested outbound operations at three ports of entry on the southwest border. Our investigators observed that CBP officers and Border Patrol agents were interviewing travelers, inspecting vehicles, and performing secondary inspections at each port.[49] At each of these locations, our investigators bypassed opportunities to turn around and proceeded on a traffic lane at the entrance to the port of entry marked as the route to Mexico, signaling their intent to leave the country. They entered a designated outbound inspection area with shredded cash hidden in the trunk of their car.[50] At two of the three ports of entry our investigators claimed that they only wanted to see the border and would like to turn around when approached by CBP officers and Border Patrol agents conducting outbound inspections. At both of these ports of entry, officers and agents allowed the investigators to turn around without searching the vehicle, asking for identification, or probing further to determine whether our investigators posed a risk of smuggling. In addition, the officers and agents did not question our investigators on why they did not turn around earlier when they had an opportunity to do so. At the third port of entry, CBP officers did not interview our investigators or physically inspect the vehicle that contained the shredded cash. However, CBP officers used an X-ray detector on the vehicle.

Program Data, Policies and Procedures, and Performance Measures Could Be Strengthened to Improve the Outbound Program

Addressing the limitations described above could require substantial capital investments at all ports of entry. However, the extent that such investments could result in greater seizures of bulk cash, weapons and ammunition is not known, in part because CBP lacks data on benefits and costs of an expanded program. CBP will likely need more time to gain a clearer understanding of how well the program is working and what factors will contribute most to improved results. Data on the expected costs and benefits of the program are a basic building block for informing decisions on whether to expand the program, continue the program at current levels, or to reduce the size of the program. In addition, policies and procedures to ensure the safety of officers are not in place. CBP has developed strategic goals for its outbound program, but it lacks performance measures that assess the effectiveness of the program.

Limited Data on Expected Program Costs and Benefits Hinders CBP's Ability to Inform Decisions on the Budget and Outbound Program

As the outbound program matures, developing additional cost data in four key areas—staffing, technology, infrastructure, and wait times created by outbound operations—could help inform decisionmakers on program and budget decisions. OMB provides guidance on how agencies can evaluate the costs and benefits of a program, such as the Outbound Enforcement Program, to inform policymakers on budget and program decisions.[51] In addition, DHS calls on its components to carry out analyses of costs and benefits to assist in planning a project and in managing costs and risks.[52] The Southwest Border Counternarcotics Strategy states that law enforcement agencies should analyze the effectiveness of outbound inspections and, if warranted, consider expanding the number of inspections in search of bulk currency.[53]

Data for Determining Staffing Costs for Expanded Operations Has Limits

While CBP has data on the current cost of the Outbound Enforcement Program, it faces challenges in developing cost data to estimate the future size of the program. From fiscal years 2008 through 2010, the cost of CBP's outbound program increased from about $89 million to an estimated $145 million. Costs for the outbound program involved primarily the cost of headquarters and mission support staff as well as salaries, benefits, overtime and premium pay for officers. Together these items represent more than 98 percent of the total cost for each fiscal year. Appendix I provides a more detailed breakdown of costs for the outbound program.

CBP plans to improve its data for estimating the cost of staff involved in inspecting outbound traffic for its current level of effort. For example, CBP plans to refine the data by calling on CBP managers at ports of entry to estimate the total number of hours officers worked during an outbound shift rather than simply counting the number of officers who worked that day.

While CBP has cost data for staffing the current level of effort, challenges remain for estimating costs of staffing the program in the future. CBP has developed an Outbound Workload Staffing Model to assist managers in determining future staffing levels. However, the model has data limitations, in part, because data on outbound operations is limited or missing because the program is new. For example, the model does not identify the number of CBP canine handlers that are needed to support outbound operations. Having such data would inform future iterations of the model in estimating the number of currency canine handlers that may be needed. Also, the model assumes that outbound traffic volumes are the same as inbound traffic volumes because CBP does not have data on the number of travelers and vehicles that leave the country through land ports of entry. According to these staff, having such data would be helpful in determining staffing needs.

CBP is Making Progress in Developing Cost Estimates of Equipment Needed by CBP Officers to Carry Out Outbound Operations at Land Ports of Entry

CBP managers stated that they are developing a list of equipment officers need to conduct outbound operations at land ports of entry. Such a list would include equipment, such as mirrors, fiber-optic scopes, and density readers that CBP officers need to inspect vehicles leaving the country. Managers stated that they plan to develop the initial list by the end of 2010 and they would submit the list to managers at ports of entry for comment in 2011. Once comments have been received, CBP plans to develop a cost estimate for outbound equipment later in 2011.

One source of funding for purchasing equipment by CBP is the Department of the Treasury's Forfeiture Fund. In fiscal year 2009, CBP deposited more than $25 million into the fund from currency forfeitures. CBP is permitted by the Department of the Treasury's Executive Office of Asset Forfeiture to use money from the fund to purchase equipment and infrastructure such as canopies, signage and lighting to support outbound operations.[54] However, CBP has expressed concern about using the funds for a one-time purchase of equipment and infrastructure because funding is not available for maintenance and repair of the equipment in the CBP Office of Field Operations budget. For fiscal year 2010, CBP requested $7.5 million so that the agency could pay overtime to state and local law enforcement officers who work outbound operations with CBP at ports of entry and $500 thousand for equipment, such as currency counters, digital cameras, and contraband detection kits. In total, CBP requested about $102 million from the Treasury Forfeiture Fund for fiscal year 2010. As of June 2010, CBP had received almost $55 million from the fund, however, none of this money was for the outbound program.

CBP is Making Progress in Developing Cost Estimates of Technology Improvements

CBP has a project underway to determine how to upgrade and install license plate readers and to enable computer connectivity, but the agency has not yet determined how much this would cost at each port. According to CBP, license plate readers are available at 48 of 118 outbound lanes on the southwest border and none of the 179 outbound lanes on the northern border. Additionally, CBP officials estimated that there are a limited number of outbound lanes networked to support computer stations or wireless computing, both necessary for document readers that we discussed earlier in this report. CBP officials in charge of the project stated that they plan to determine the costs involved in deploying license plate readers and computer connectivity and that a cost estimate will be available in September 2010. Such estimates could provide important information for CBP outbound program managers as they assess scenarios for outbound operations at each port of entry.

Cost Estimates of Infrastructure Improvements Are Limited

Although CBP has plans to consider outbound infrastructure needs, it has not yet conducted an analysis of outbound infrastructure needs at ports of entry and the related costs for improving infrastructure for its outbound operations. The strategic plan for the Outbound Enforcement Program states that the program will request the necessary budgetary funding to conduct facility assessments at ports of entry and articulate the operational needs for outbound facilities. CBP has completed a preliminary assessment of Southwestern ports of entry in which it determined the readiness of each site to accommodate outbound infrastructure. However, this preliminary assessment did not estimate the costs of infrastructure improvements at each port of entry. Building on this effort, CBP plans to conduct a site survey that would consider needed infrastructure at each port of entry and stakeholders that would be involved in construction such as local governments and private landholders. However, Outbound Enforcement Division officials told us in July 2010, that they will not begin to conduct site surveys until they receive funds for construction. They have not requested this funding because DHS has not yet determined whether to expand the program. Without cost estimates, it will be difficult for CBP to inform program managers and policymakers about costs involved in improving infrastructure for the Outbound Enforcement Program.

Developing Data on the Costs Created by Wait Times Is a Difficult Task

In its Circular A-94 guidance, OMB states that agencies should consider all costs of a program when conducting a cost-benefit analysis, such as the costs resulting from waiting at the border. CBP officials told us that they have not yet collected data on wait times for outbound inspections because they have been initially focused on establishing the program.[55] Furthermore, they said that developing cost data on wait times for outbound inspections would be difficult based on CBP's experiences in collecting similar wait time data for inbound inspections.

In July 2010, we reported that CBP's wait times data for personal and commercial vehicles in inbound inspections are collected using inconsistent methods and the data are unreliable. CBP acknowledged problems with its wait times data and has initiated a pilot project to automate wait times measurement, and to improve the accuracy and consistency of the data collected. The objectives of the project are to measure wait times in both directions—inbound and outbound—for cars and trucks, determine real-time and predictive capabilities, replace the manual process for calculating wait times, and explore long-term operations.[56] Understanding what kinds of delays might result from outbound inspections and how expanding the program might affect such delays could better position CBP in determining the program's costs.

Analyzing Seizure Data and Other Benefits of Outbound Operations Is Challenging

While seizure data are useful for determining many of the benefits of outbound operations, some benefits are more difficult to quantify. For example, it is difficult to quantify the degree to which outbound operations deter drug trafficking organizations from attempting to smuggle bulk cash. Another benefit that is difficult to quantify is the intelligence information that officers may obtain by conducting outbound operations, including information that may help in discovering smuggled cash, weapons and drugs. To address this type of difficulty, OMB encourages agencies to enumerate any other benefits beyond those that can be quantified.[57] For example, agencies that have conducted such analyses have used subject matter experts to offer a qualitative evaluation of benefits.

In analyzing the costs and benefits of the outbound inspections program, it is important to recognize that CBP is part of a larger effort by federal, state, and local agencies to disrupt and dismantle drug trafficking organizations, in part by denying them the profits of their drug sales. How much CBP spends to combat such activities could be indirectly affected by the efforts of other agencies involved in interdiction activities. For example, if local police officers were to increase enforcement on highways leading to the border, they may intercept bulk cash before it gets to the border, potentially changing the results of CBP's efforts. Additionally, if CBP increases its outbound operations, criminals may respond to the increased difficulty of smuggling bulk cash by changing tactics to use other means of moving currency out of the country, such as using stored value. We discuss the use of stored value later in this report.

CBP's Outbound Policies and Procedures Do Not Address Weaknesses Related to Officer Safety

CBP has not yet developed policies and procedures to help ensure officer safety in conducting outbound operations. At all five ports of entry we visited, CBP officers and managers cited safety concerns related to conducting outbound inspections. In addition, at each of these ports, we observed that officers used the side of the highway to conduct secondary inspections, while other vehicles moved past, potentially endangering officers. Also, at the Blaine port of entry, the officers conducted inspections of the underside of vehicles in the traffic by lying on the ground with their legs exposed while traffic moved by in neighboring lanes at speeds up to approximately 25 miles per hour.

CBP program managers noted that one way to improve the safety of officers is to improve infrastructure, such as developing designated areas for secondary inspections and installing speed bumps and barriers. We agree that improved infrastructure could enhance officer safety, however, whether CBP will receive funds to improve infrastructure remains an open question. Until such improvements are made, CBP will be faced with the important issue of how to ensure officer safety.

At two of the five ports of entry we visited, CBP was using guidance for outbound operations that was developed prior to the reestablishment of the Outbound Enforcement Program and it does not specify how CBP officers should inspect travelers in a way that ensures the officers' safety. This guidance states that the safety of teams conducting outbound operations is an important consideration, but otherwise does not provide safety guidance for officers. At two other ports of entry we visited, CBP officials stated that the ports began conducting outbound operations after the Outbound Enforcement Program was reestablished but did not reference any specific guidance for officers to use. At the Laredo port of entry, officials provided us with locally developed guidance for officers that details specific actions that the officers should take to help ensure their safety. For example, the officer should always face the traffic, use loud commands to vehicles when escorting a vehicle to secondary screening, and remain aware of traffic passing him or her.

At the time of this report, CBP had not yet issued an outbound directive to ports of entry that provides guidance for ensuring officer safety. In July 2010, a CBP outbound program manager told us that a directive for the program was under review by CBP management; however the official could not provide estimates on when the directive is to be approved and issued. The manager agreed that policies and procedures on officer safety are important. However, the manager said that developing such policies and procedures should be done at the local level because each port of entry is unique. For example, traffic volumes vary for each port of entry. The manager stated that the draft directive does not include guidance that directs managers at land ports of entry to develop policies and procedures for ensuring officer safety. GAO's *Standards for Internal Control in the Federal Government* state that policies and procedures enforce management directives and help ensure that actions are taken to address risks. In addition, the standards state that such control activities are an integral part of an entity's planning, implementing, reviewing, and accountability for stewardship of government resources and achieving effective results.[58] Directing and ensuring that managers at ports of entry develop policies and procedures for officer safety could help protect officers from danger when they are conducting outbound operations.

CBP Has Developed Strategic Goals for Its Outbound Enforcement Program, but Challenges Remain in Developing Measures Related to Program Effectiveness

In October 2009, CBP issued a strategic plan for fiscal years 2010 through 2014 that represented a first step toward developing performance measures for outbound efforts, but challenges remain in developing the measures. The plan states that the immediate goal of the program was to obstruct the illegal flow of firearms and currency being smuggled from the United States to drug trafficking organizations in Mexico. According to the plan, a key objective of CBP's outbound efforts is to detect and remove people and goods that pose a threat from the legitimate annual flow of millions of people, cargo and conveyances departing from the United States. To help achieve this objective, the Outbound Enforcement Program plans to carry out 11 initiatives, such as conducting an outbound threat assessment and tracking and reporting on outbound activities.[59]

The strategic plan for the outbound program also recognizes that developing or obtaining better data on the threat of bulk cash smuggling and other illegal activities is one key to understanding the effectiveness of its operations. For example, the outbound program recognizes the value of assessments that identify major trafficking routes and methods for illegal export activities. However, CBP has yet to develop a performance measure that shows the degree to which its efforts are stemming the flow of bulk cash leaving the country. While we recognize that doing so is a difficult task, we reported in September 2005 that agencies can use performance information to inform decisions on future strategies, planning and budgeting, and allocating resources.[60] In addition, *Standards for Internal Control in the Federal Government* state that control activities, such as establishing and reviewing performance measures, are an integral part of an entity's planning, implementing, reviewing and accountability for stewardship of government resources and achieving effective results.[61] Such activities could call for comparisons and assessments relating different sets of data to one another so that analyses of the relationships can be made and appropriate actions can be taken.

Using information and data from other agencies that evaluate drug trafficking organizations provides one way to measure the effectiveness of CBP's outbound operations. Two examples of how such information could inform managers and policymakers of CBP's efforts involve studies by NDIC and ICE. In March 2008, NDIC estimated that while current bulk cash interdiction efforts successfully disrupt the transport of tens of millions of dollars in drug proceeds en route to or at the southwest border every year, the interdicted currency is less than 1 percent of the total amount of illicit bulk cash destined for Mexico.[62] In addition, a November 2009 study issued by ICE stated that gross revenue generated by Mexican drug trafficking organizations, and subsequently smuggled into Mexico, is substantial.[63] CBP officials stated that while it may not be possible to know the extent to which its officers are intercepting cash, they believe such information is useful. For example, they cited analyses by ICE's Bulk Cash Smuggling Center as another data source that could help in developing performance measures.[64] In July 2010, CBP officials stated that they plan to develop draft performance measures comparing program costs to outcomes such as the amount of bulk cash seized by the end of fiscal year 2011. While this is a good first step, without data to show the degree to which CBP efforts are stemming bulk cash smuggling and other criminal activities, it will be difficult for managers and policymakers to assess the effectiveness of CBP's outbound program.

Regulatory Gaps Involving Cross- Border Reporting and Other Anti-Money Laundering Requirements Exist for Stored Value

Regardless of the success of efforts to stem the flow of bulk cash, criminals can use other methods of transporting proceeds from illegal activities across the nation's borders. Stored value is one such method. [65] Regulatory exemptions heighten the risk that criminals may use stored value to finance their operations. For example, unlike cash, FinCEN does not require travelers to report stored value in excess of $10,000 to CBP when crossing the border. FinCEN has initiated actions to address these exemptions, but much work remains before the regulatory gaps are closed and anti-money laundering practices are fully implemented.

Unlike with Cash, Travelers Are Not Required to Report More than $10,000 in Stored Value When Crossing the U.S. Border

The Bank Secrecy Act (BSA) is a key federal statute that seeks to safeguard the U.S. financial system from criminal activity and to combat the exploitation of the U.S. financial system by criminals and terrorists. Among other things, the BSA authorizes the Secretary of the Treasury to require financial institutions, as well as non-financial trades or businesses and many individuals, to make reports and maintain records that have a high degree of usefulness in criminal, tax, or regulatory investigations or proceedings, or in the conduct of intelligence or counterintelligence activities, including analysis, to protect against international terrorism.[66] Among other things, the BSA and its current implementing regulations require an individual who physically transports, mails, or ships more than $10,000 in currency or monetary instruments, such as traveler's checks, across the U.S. border to file a Report of International Transportation of Currency or Monetary Instrument (CMIR).[67]

Unlike this reporting requirement for currency and monetary instruments, there is no similar requirement for stored value. According to Treasury, no requirement exists because stored value is not defined as a monetary instrument under the BSA or its implementing regulations. Instead, according to FinCEN, stored value is a device that provides access to monetary value, rather than being a monetary instrument itself.

MSBs That Issue, Sell, or Redeem Stored Value Are Exempt from Three Key Anti-Money Laundering Provisions of the BSA[68]

Many of the anti-money laundering requirements contained in the BSA regulations do not apply to MSBs that offer stored value products. The BSA and its regulatory framework focus on financial institutions' record keeping and reporting requirements that create a paper trail of financial transactions that federal agencies can use to deter criminal activity and apprehend criminals. Some BSA regulations apply to MSBs that offer stored value products. For example, financial institutions, including MSBs that provide stored value products, are required to report currency transactions made by the same customer that exceed $10,000 during the course of any one day. [69]

However, FinCEN exempted MSBs that offer stored value products from many other anti-money laundering provisions of the BSA regulations.[70]

According to FinCEN, they provided these exemptions in their 1999 rulemaking due to the "complexity of the industry and the desire to avoid unintended consequences with respect to an industry then in its infancy."[71] In 2008, FinCEN recognized that these exemptions created a situation whereby issuers, sellers, and redeemers of stored value are subject to a less comprehensive Bank Secrecy Act/Anti-Money Laundering regime than are other actors falling within the scope of FinCEN's regulations. FinCEN later stated that "if these [regulatory] gaps are not addressed, there is increased potential for the use of [stored value] as a means for furthering money laundering, terrorist financing, and other illicit transactions through the financial system."[72] Below is a discussion of three key exemptions related to stored value activity by MSBs. We discuss FinCEN's efforts to address these exemptions later in the report.

FinCEN Does Not Require MSBs That Are Sole Issuers, Sellers, or Redeemers of Stored Value to Register

Under the BSA and its implementing regulations, certain MSBs must register with Treasury by filing information with FinCEN.[73] The purpose of registration is to assist supervisory and law enforcement agencies in th e enforcement of criminal, tax, and regulatory laws and to prevent MSBs from engaging in illegal activities. [74] While most types of MSBs are required to register, there are exemptions for certain types of MSBs. For example, a MSB that solely issues, sells, or redeems stored value is not required to register under current BSA regulations.[75] The total number of MSBs that are solely issuers, sellers, or redeemers of stored value, and thus exempt from registration, is unknown.

A MSB that issues, sells, or redeems stored value is generally required to register with FinCEN if that MSB also provides another financial service which is subject to registration, such as check cashing. However, in 2007, the Secretaries of the Treasury and Homeland Security, and the Attorney General, stated that the majority of MSBs that are required to register continue to operate without doing so.[76] According to FinCEN officials, roughly 25,000 MSBs were registered in May 2007. Through an outreach program to unregistered MSBs, FinCEN increased the number of registered MSBs to 43,041, as of June 15, 2010. However, the total number of MSBs operating nationwide is unknown.[77,78] FinCEN officials stated that MSBs may not register because of language barriers, cost, training issues, or a lack of awareness as to the requirements.

FinCEN Does Not Specifically Require MSBs to Develop and Implement a Customer Identification Program

Under BSA regulations, some financial institutions, such as banks, are required to have customer identification programs that include, among other things, procedures for verifying customer identity and determining whether a customer appears on specified government watch lists. However, current BSA regulations do not specifically require MSBs to have a customer identification program. Despite this, MSBs may choose to implement customer identification protocols voluntarily or in order to satisfy other requirements.[79] For example, MSBs are required to maintain anti-money laundering programs. These programs are designed to prevent the MSB from being used to facilitate money laundering and the financing of terrorist activities. As part of this requirement, MSBs are required to develop and implement policies, procedures, and internal controls which include, to the extent applicable to the MSBs under BSA regulations, requirements for verifying customer identification.[80] We discuss FinCEN's efforts to monitor MSB compliance with these requirements later in this report.

For law enforcement agencies, having records and documents on the individual who carries out the transactions is a key step in their ability to successfully investigate cross-border currency smuggling and other illegal activity. For example, a threat assessment of stored value cards by Treasury stated the following:

- "The 9/11 hijackers opened U.S. bank accounts, had face-to-face dealings with bank employees, signed signature cards and received wire transfers, all of which left financial footprints. Law enforcement was able to follow the trail, identify the hijackers and trace them back to their terror cells and confederates abroad. Had the 9/11 terrorists used prepaid [stored value] cards to cover their expenses, none of these financial footprints would have been available."[81]

FinCEN Does Not Require MSBs to Report Suspicious Transactions Involving Stored Value

While depository institutions are required to file suspicious activity reports (SAR) for stored value transactions, FinCEN does not require MSBs to do so.[82, 83, 84] Although some MSBs may file SARs related to stored value as part of their anti-money laundering programs or on a voluntary basis, the fact that suspicious activity involving stored value does not have to be reported by all financial institutions heightens the risk that cross-border currency smuggling or the illegal use of stored value may go undetected or unreported.

Suspicious activity reports inform the federal government of any suspicious transaction related to a possible violation of law or regulation, such as money laundering, and can be a valuable source of information for federal agencies involved in detecting, deterring, and apprehending criminals. For example, in February 2009, we reported that law enforcement agencies in the Department of Justice and DHS use SARs in their investigations of money laundering, terrorist financing, and other financial crimes.[85] In one example, a bank-filed SAR began an investigation that resulted in the discovery of a predatory certificate of deposit fraud scheme. The SAR narrative described critical elements of the crime in detail and law enforcement and prosecutors in this case noted that the SAR proved instrumental in ending the scheme.

FinCEN has determined that suspicious activities related to stored value have been reported by depository institutions and voluntarily reported by MSBs. For example, in 2006, FinCEN conducted an analysis of SARs that identified stored value cards as the nexus of the suspicious activity in order to highlight trends and patterns associated with the questionable/criminal use of stored value cards. FinCEN found that between January 1, 2004, and February 15, 2006, 471 SARs were filed that were associated with stored value activity.[86] Of these, 341 SARs (72 percent), generally described activities associated with structuring and/or money laundering.[87]

Law Enforcement Case Examples and Reported Suspicious Activities Demonstrate the Use of Stored Value for Cross-Border Currency Smuggling and Other Illicit Activities

In its 2010 report on bi-national criminal proceeds led by the Office of Counternarcotics Enforcement and ICE, DHS reported that little is known about whether Mexican criminal enterprises are making use of stored value technologies. Further, it reported that intelligence gaps center around a lack of data on emerging technologies like stored value cards, especially those that are offshore based.[88] However, in a March 2010 testimony before the House Appropriations Committee, the FBI Director stated that recent money laundering investigations demonstrate that criminals are able to exploit existing vulnerabilities in the reporting requirements in order to move criminal proceeds using stored value devices, such as prepaid cards.

While the extent to which stored value is used for illicit purposes is unknown, law enforcement case examples and reported suspicious activities demonstrate that stored value has been used for cross-border currency smuggling and other illicit activities.[89] At least two mechanisms that can be used to move currency out of the country using stored value devices have been documented by law enforcement and reported suspicious activities. First, illegal proceeds can be loaded on stored value devices and physically carried across the border. Two examples of the physical transport of stored value across the U.S. border are described below.

- CBP officers at a Washington state port of entry stopped a commercial shipping truck and discovered $7.2 million worth of prepaid phone cards. CBP officers report that they were unable to detain or seize these phone cards because there is no requirement that such cards be reported at the border. Later analysis revealed the manufacturer had sent five other shipments of phone cards across the border in a 3- month period, totaling more than $25 million.
- ICE agents assisting with outbound inspections at the San Ysidro port of entry encountered an individual attempting to leave the country in possession of a laptop computer, several merchandise gift cards, credit cards, and cell phones. Upon further investigation, the agents uncovered that the passenger had over 1,000 stolen credit card numbers and was working as part of a credit card fraud operation. The passenger explained that for his work, he was paid with prepaid gift cards. The man used these gift cards to purchase prepaid phone cards, which he smuggled into Mexico and sold for a profit.

The second method involves moving illicit proceeds out of the country by shipping stored value cards out of the country, where co-conspirators can use the cards to make purchases or to withdraw cash from local ATMs. Many cards can also be reloaded with additional value remotely via the Internet. For example, in 2008, DEA agents in Connecticut were investigating a narcotics and money laundering organization allegedly using stored value cards to launder narcotics proceeds. The investigation revealed that illicit proceeds were loaded onto stored value cards, which were then shipped to Colombia, South America. In Colombia, coconspirators withdrew the money from local ATMs. The investigation revealed that in a 5-month period, conspirators withdrew more than $7 million from the stored value cards at a single location in Medellin, Colombia.

As discussed above, stored value devices are not subject to cross-border reporting requirements. As a result, individuals are not required to file any report if they physically transport, mail, or ship more than $10,000 in value in the form of stored value products. Four of six law enforcement agencies with whom we spoke expressed concern about the lack of a cross-border transport reporting requirement for stored value.[90] For example, CBP senior officials report that because stored value is not subject to CMIR requirements, they lack the authority to seize stored value devices at the border without establishing probable cause or linking the stored value devices to a specified unlawful activity. In contrast, an IRS special agent told us that a cross-border reporting requirement would not entirely address the illicit use of stored value because there are other mechanisms by which stored value can be used to transport funds internationally. For example, smugglers could physically carry or ship stored value cards with no value out of the country and then add value to the cards remotely.

Beyond the use of stored value for cross-border currency smuggling, law enforcement examples and reported suspicious activities demonstrate that stored value can be used for other illicit purposes, such as money laundering, tax fraud, and identity theft. Below are two examples:

- In a recent law enforcement case, stored value cards were used to conceal proceeds of a $15 million tax fraud scheme. In this example, suspects filed more than 540 fraudulent tax returns. On some occasions, the suspects routed electronic transfers of tax refunds directly to prepaid cards obtained anonymously through an Internet application process.
- A depository institution filed a suspicious activity report describing a customer who loaded $73,405 on one prepaid card and $9,987 on a second prepaid card over the course of about a year and a half. All transactions were made in cash, mostly $20 bills, and reporting officials noted that the cash had an odor similar to marijuana. Of the $73,405 loaded on the card, $72,212 was withdrawn in cash. While the deposits took place in Washington state, the transactions on the card occurred in Southern California and Mexico.

EFFORTS ARE UNDER WAY TO ADDRESS REGULATORY GAPS RELATED TO STORED VALUE, BUT MUCH WORK REMAINS

FinCEN Is in the Process of Developing and Issuing Regulations that Require Anti-Money Laundering Practices for Stored Value

At the time of our review, FinCEN was in the process of developing and issuing regulations, as required by the Credit CARD Act,[91] to address the risk associated with the illicit use of stored value. On May 22, 2009, the Credit CARD Act was enacted which, among other things, required the Secretary of the Treasury, in consultation with the Secretary of Homeland Security, to do the following:

- Issue regulations in final form implementing the BSA, regarding the sale, issuance, redemption, or international transport of stored value, including stored value cards. In doing so, the Credit CARD Act stated that Treasury may issue regulations regarding the international transport of stored value to include reporting requirements pursuant to 31 U.S.C. § 5316 which applies to the transport of monetary instruments.[92]
- Take into consideration current and future needs and methodologies for transmitting and storing value in electronic form in developing the regulations.

The Credit CARD Act also called on Treasury to issue final regulations implementing the above requirements by February 2010.[93] FinCEN is in the early phases of issuing the related regulations and much work remains before it addresses the risk of cross-border currency smuggling and money laundering through the use of stored value.[94] For significant regulatory action, such as the proposed rule that FinCEN developed on stored value, OMB prescribes an 11-step process.[95] This process involves steps that range from drafting a Notice of Proposed Rulemaking (NPRM) to publication of the final rule at least 60 days before its effective date. In June 2010, FinCEN issued a NPRM. FinCEN proposes to revise the BSA regulations applicable to MSBs with regard to stored value by, among other things, renaming "stored value" as "prepaid access" and defining that term; imposing suspicious activity reporting requirements, customer information and transaction recordkeeping requirements on providers and sellers of prepaid access; and imposing a registration requirement on providers of prepaid access. [96]

In preparing the NPRM, FinCEN carried out several actions. For example, FinCEN consulted with Treasury components, such as IRS SB/SE and IRS-Criminal Investigations Divisions. In addition, it obtained input from external stakeholders including industry, law enforcement, and federal agencies and departments. In doing so, FinCEN officials told us they consulted with and obtained input from DHS agencies, such as ICE and CBP, before and after writing versions of the draft rule.[97] In addition, FinCEN received comments from OMB prior to issuing the NPRM.

Treasury and FinCEN officials told us that they accelerated their efforts toward developing and issuing a new rule on stored value due in part to the requirements under the Credit CARD Act. They acknowledged that the existing regulations for stored value—issued in 1999—have not kept pace with developments in the stored value industry and that the regulations were now outdated. However, agency officials said they believe that their efforts prior to the Credit CARD Act, such as leading an interagency effort to develop and issue the 2007 Money Laundering Strategy Report, establishing a Stored Value Subcommittee of the Bank Secrecy Act Advisory Group in May 2008, and posing questions related to stored value to the public as part of proposed revisions to MSB definitions in May 2009,[98] placed them in a better position to establish a regulatory framework for stored value in response to the Credit CARD Act.

We describe in more detail below how FinCEN plans to address several of the regulatory gaps that apply to MSBs involved in stored value. However, FinCEN has not established an end date for the regulations, which is discussed later in this report.

FinCEN Proposes Addressing Three Regulatory Gaps Related to MSBs Involved in Stored Value

Recognizing that stored value products are vulnerable to money laundering, FinCEN's June 2010 NPRM proposes to address regulatory gaps related to MSBs involved in stored value or "prepaid access" in the following three areas:

- *Registration with FinCEN.* The NPRM proposes that providers of prepaid access must (1) register with FinCEN as a MSB,[99] (2) identify each prepaid program for which it is the provider of prepaid access, and (3) maintain a list of its agents. However, sellers, such as grocery stores or drug stores, of prepaid access would not have to register.[100] According to FinCEN, it is proposing to exempt the seller from registering with FinCEN because the seller's role is complementary with, but not equal to, the authority and primacy of the provider of prepaid access, and the seller is generally acting as an agent on behalf of the provider. As stated in the NPRM, providing an exemption would be consistent with the treatment of other agents under the MSB rules.

- *Customer identification program.* The NPRM proposes that providers and sellers of prepaid access must establish procedures to verify the identity of a person who obtains prepaid access under a prepaid program; obtain identifying information concerning such a person, including name, date of birth, address, and identification number; and retain such identifying information for 5 years after the termination of the relationship.
- *Submitting reports on suspicious activities.* The NPRM proposes that MSBs must file reports on suspicious activities related to prepaid access.[101]

The next steps that FinCEN plans to follow include (1) summarizing and analyzing the comments, (2) revising the regulation as proposed in the NPRM, if appropriate, (3) consulting with law enforcement and regulatory stakeholders and clearance within Treasury, (4) preparing a final rule for OMB to review, and (5) addressing any further comments from OMB.

FinCEN Has Not Yet Decided How Best to Address the International Transport of Stored Value

At the time of our review, FinCEN was considering several options to address the international transport of stored value; however, the agency has not yet decided on what course of action it will take or when. In the June 2010 NPRM, FinCEN stated that it plans to regulate the cross-border transport of stored value in a future rulemaking proposal in part because of issues identified with respect to financial transparency while performing its regulatory research of the stored value industry. According to FinCEN officials, they have not addressed the cross-border transport of stored value in the June 2010 NPRM because addressing regulatory gaps in (1) registration with FinCEN, (2) customer identification programs, and (3) reporting on suspicious activities had a higher priority.

While FinCEN may ultimately call upon individuals to report stored value at the borders, FinCEN officials indicated that cross-border transparency and monitoring may be achieved through other means. According to FinCEN, one option it may use to achieve cross-border transparency is to call upon entities in the stored value industry to report suspicious activities related to the use of stored value that cuts across the nation's borders. In addition, FinCEN is proposing in the June 2010 NPRM that providers of prepaid access maintain records that may include information on the type and amount of the transaction and the date, time, and location where the transaction occurred. For example, such information could identify the purchase and use of stored value in and outside of the United States. FinCEN's success in using this approach depends, in part, on (1) the degree to which entities report such instances in a complete and accurate fashion and (2) the timeliness of such reporting and the degree to which the information is shared with law enforcement agencies. The challenges FinCEN faces in using this approach are discussed later in this report.

FinCEN Has Developed Initial Plans for Issuing the Final Rule on Stored Value, but Its Plans Do Not Assess Ways to Mitigate Risks for Completing Rules on Stored Value

FinCEN has developed initial plans for issuing the final rules for stored value; however, its plans are missing key elements that are consistent with best practices for project management. Best practices for project management established by the Project Management Institute state that managing a project involves project risk management, which serves to increase the probability and impact of positive events, and decrease the probability and impact of events adverse to the project. Project risk management entails determining which risks might affect a project, prioritizing risks for further analysis by assessing their probability of occurrence, and developing actions to reduce threats to the project. Other practices include (1) establishing clear and achievable objectives, (2) balancing the competing demands for quality, scope, time, and cost, (3) adapting the specifications, plans, and approach to the different concerns and expectations of the various stakeholders involved in the project, and (4) developing milestone dates to identify points throughout the project to reassess efforts under way to determine whether project changes are necessary.[102]

In an effort to meet the statutory deadline of February 2010, FinCEN developed preliminary plans and milestones for issuing the final rule on stored value. For example, the agency identified certain steps in the rulemaking process, such as summarizing comments and making recommendations to management before finalizing the rule. However, FinCEN's plans did not assess which risks might affect the project, prioritize risks for further analysis by assessing their probability of occurrence, or develop actions to reduce threats to the project as suggested by best practices for project management. While FinCEN officials acknowledge risks exist, such as not knowing whether the nature of these comments may cause FinCEN to change its policy path with respect to the NPRM, they have not produced a plan that identifies actions to reduce threats to the project nor does their plan (1) consider alternative approaches that the agency may need to take based on comments received, or (2) include the time it may take to produce a series of rules, including a rule that addresses the cross-border transport of stored value. Assessing ways to mitigate risks associated with issuing rules on stored value and the cross-border transport of stored value could better position FinCEN to provide reasonable assurance that it can produce a set of rules that (1) fulfills the requirements of the Credit CARD Act and (2) informs decisions related to improving anti-money laundering practices among the stored value industry.

In general, federal rulemaking can be a lengthy process for significant regulatory action. In April 2009, we reported that the average time needed to complete a significant rulemaking across 16 case-study rules at four federal agencies[103] was about 4 years—having a range from about 1 year to nearly 14 years with considerable variation among the federal agencies and rules.[104] However, as called for by best practices for project management, all four of the federal agencies examined in the report set milestones for their regulatory development. Additionally, during the course of our review one of the four agencies provided data showing it routinely tracked these milestones, and two federal agencies subsequently provided some documentation and data to show likewise, when commenting on our draft report. Our report concluded that monitoring actual versus estimated performance enables agency managers to identify steps in the rulemaking process that account for substantial development time and provides information necessary to further evaluate whether the time was well spent.

A project management plan that is consistent with best practices could help FinCEN better manage its rulemaking effort. The Credit CARD Act required FinCEN's effort in issuing regulations in final form implementing the BSA regarding the sale, issuance, redemption, or international transport of stored value to be completed within the prescribed time frame of 270 days from the date of enactment. However, FinCEN was unable to meet the statutory deadline of February 2010 to develop and issue these regulations and has much work to do to carry out the requirements of the Credit CARD Act. In addition to identifying and mitigating risks associated with the regulatory process, a project management plan could also help FinCEN (1) track and measure progress on tasks associated with completing mandated requirements, and (2) identify points throughout the project to reassess efforts under way to determine whether goals and milestones are achievable or project changes are necessary. If such plans call for changes to time lines, then FinCEN could request for legislation to extend the statutory deadline. Until the rule is finalized and implemented, vulnerabilities could continue to exist in the stored value industry with respect to the cross-border transport of stored value and money laundering for the purpose of supporting illegal activities.

More Work Remains to Ensure Agencies Enforce Cross-Border Currency Smuggling and Industry Complies with the Final Rule

While issuing the final rule on stored value will be a major step toward addressing regulatory gaps, much work remains to ensure enforcement by law enforcement agencies to identify cross-border currency smuggling with the use of stored value and to ensure issuers, sellers, and redeemers of such devices implement anti-money laundering requirements after the final rule is issued. For example, FinCEN faces the task of conducting awareness programs about the new rule for officials in law enforcement and industry, as well as determining whether the new rule will address the Credit CARD Act requirements or if additional rules will need to be developed. Beyond these tasks, federal law enforcement agencies and FinCEN face other challenges as well. These are described in more detail below.

Enforcing the Cross-Border Requirements Related to Stored Value Will Be a Challenge

If FinCEN requires individuals to declare stored value at the border when leaving the country, law enforcement officials we spoke to report that they would encounter the following challenges.

- *Detecting illegitimate stored value cards.* According to the law enforcement officials we spoke with, it may be difficult to detect illegitimate stored value for three reasons. First, stored value cards loaded with large amounts of currency can be easily concealed in a wallet, letter, or package given the minimal amount of physical space a stored value product occupies, particularly when compared to bulk cash. Second, stored value cards do not contain any features that distinguish them from traditional credit or debit cards. Third, there is no mechanism by which to distinguish stored value cards that an individual possesses for legitimate reasons and those possessed for illegitimate reasons.

- *Obtaining proper traveler declarations*. The public would have to be made aware of any new declaration requirement for the international transport of stored value. Further, it may be difficult for the traveler to recall the value on a stored value card and for law enforcement to verify the value on a card. Unlike cash which can be counted, the value of a stored value card can only be determined using a card reader or by accessing the account information.
- *Seizing the funds*. Unlike cash, which can be physically seized, the process of seizing funds from a stored value card is much more difficult. Law enforcement first has to identify where the funds are held, which could be at any financial institution worldwide. Second, law enforcement would need to obtain the right to freeze the funds and to seize the funds through obtaining a warrant. However, in the time it takes to obtain a warrant, it is possible that a suspect and any coconspirators could transfer the funds off of the stored value card to another account.

FinCEN Faces Challenges in Ensuring Industry Compliance with the New Rules

FinCEN's approach for addressing vulnerabilities with cross-border currency smuggling and other illicit use of stored value depends, in part, on ensuring that industry complies with the new rules. Among other things, FinCEN faces challenges in areas such as monitoring MSBs, addressing gaps in anti-money laundering practices of off-shore issuers and sellers of stored value, and educating industry about the new anti- money laundering requirements.

Current Guidance for Monitoring MSB Compliance With Anti-Money Laundering Requirements Is Silent on Stored Value

As administrator of the BSA, FinCEN is responsible for, among others things, developing regulatory policies for agencies that examine financial institutions and businesses for compliance with the BSA regulations. FinCEN is also responsible for overseeing agency compliance examination activities and provides these agencies with assistance to ensure they are able to carry out their compliance exams. Treasury, through FinCEN, has delegated the authority to conduct compliance examinations of certain nonfederally regulated nonbank financial institutions (NBFI), including MSBs, to the Office of Fraud/BSA, within IRS' Small Business/Self-Employed Division. IRS Fraud/BSA carries out this function with approximately 385 field examiners nationwide.

FinCEN's guidance for these examiners lacks specific information to follow when assessing MSB compliance by issuers, sellers, and redeemers of stored value. To provide guidance for performing MSB examinations to these examiners, in December 2008, FinCEN issued, jointly with IRS, the *Bank Secrecy Act/Anti-Money Laundering Examination Manual For Money Services Businesses*.[105] FinCEN's goal was to ensure consistency in the application of the anti-money laundering requirements called for by BSA. The manual includes general procedures that are applicable to all MSBs, such as procedures for reviewing an anti-money laundering program, but it does not specifically address transaction testing procedures for examining issuers, sellers and redeemers of stored value. *Standards for Internal Controls in the Federal Government* state that an effective control environment is a key method to help agency managers achieve program objectives.[106] The standards state, among other things, that agencies should have policies and procedures that enforce management's directives. The standards also state that such control activities are an integral part of an entity's planning, implementing, reviewing, and accountability for stewardship of government resources and achieving effective results. Developing policies and procedures for monitoring entities that issue, sell, and redeem stored value could help ensure that such entities carry out current and future anti-money laundering requirements. IRS Fraud/BSA officials acknowledged that there are no specific transaction testing procedures in the manual for examiners to follow at a MSB that issues, sells, and redeems stored value. They told us that at the time the manual was developed, FinCEN did not have sufficient information on the stored value industry and it wanted to get a better understanding of the industry before including examination procedures in the manual. In July 2010, FinCEN told us that it intends to update the manual to reflect final rules on MSB re-definitions and prepaid access. However, it is uncertain when it will do so because the manual update is contingent on completion of the final rules.

FinCEN Faces Challenges in Tracking Reports on Suspicious Activities Related to Stored Value

FinCEN faces challenges regarding the ease in which it can analyze the SAR database for reports related to stored value.[107] We sought to identify the types of reported suspicious activities involving stored value or prepaid products by analyzing the SAR database; however, we experienced significant data challenges that limited our efforts. Currently, SAR forms do not contain a mechanism to indicate that stored value was the financial service involved in the suspicious activity, aside from including this information in the narrative portion of the form. Therefore, to identify SARs potentially involving stored value products, the narrative portion of the form must be searched using key terms, such as "stored value," "prepaid card," or "gift card," that might indicate this activity.[108]

We reviewed a random, probability sample of 400 SARs that were identified by using narrative search terms believed to identify SARs filed due to stored value.[109] However, for an estimated 39 percent of the reports, the suspicious activity described did not involve the use of stored value, even though one of the key search terms appeared in the narrative. For example, the search term identified in the narrative did not describe the type of suspicious activity that occurred, but rather, was included in a description of the type of services the reporting entity offered. In another example, the SAR was filed for suspicion of credit card fraud or structuring but the report also described the type of transactions the customer completed, one of which might have been the purchase of gift cards.

Due to these database limitations, it is difficult to track and monitor suspicious activity and the risks related to the use of stored value. *Standards for Internal Controls in the Federal Government* state that internal controls should include an assessment of the risks the agency faces from both external and internal sources. This guidance defines risk assessment as the identification and analysis of relevant risks associated with achieving the agency's objectives and forming a basis for determining how risks should be managed. In addition, internal control standards state that once risks have been identified, they should be analyzed for their possible effect. Risk analysis includes estimating the risk's significance, assessing the likelihood of its occurrence, and deciding how to manage the risk and what actions should be taken.

To address the difficulty in tracking suspicious activities related to stored value, FinCEN has discussed SAR form revisions with the Data Management Council that include check boxes for the types of items involved in the suspicious activity, including prepaid products. FinCEN plans to implement a revised SAR form with these changes in fiscal year 2012. Making such changes could better position FinCEN to fully evaluate the potential impact of the stored value industry on their ability to carry out the agency's broad mission of enhancing U.S. national security, deterring and detecting criminal activity, and safeguarding financial systems from abuse.

FinCEN Faces Challenges in Developing a More Complete Database of MSBs

FinCEN does not have a complete database on MSBs, including those that issue, sell, and redeem stored value. The lack of a comprehensive database complicates FinCEN's ability to educate all MSBs and other entities about the new rule and its anti-money laundering requirements since the agency does not have full knowledge of the MSB population[110] or other entities involved with stored value such as the telecommunications industry (mobile devices—cellular phones and other wireless communication devices). These entities may not be as familiar with BSA anti-money laundering requirements and need more time and orientation to understand and meet the new requirements.

Historically, identifying the population of MSBs subject to BSA requirements has been a challenge for FinCEN and IRS Fraud/BSA. This challenge has been well-documented over the years by, among others, Treasury's Inspector General,[111] us,[112] and, more recently in the 2007 National Money Laundering Strategy Report.[113] To illustrate this problem, IRS Fraud/BSA uses its Web-based Currency and Banking Retrieval System, public and commercial databases, Internet searches, and the yellow pages to identify MSBs to monitor because a complete database of MSBs does not exist. FinCEN performed searches of past BSA reports and got referrals from other law enforcement officials about potential MSBs to monitor. However, not all of the businesses identified were actually subject to BSA requirements. FinCEN officials told us they plan to use the Bank Secrecy Act Advisory Group and its Subcommittees, including the Stored Value Subcommittee, to identify ways to perform appropriate outreach to applicable MSBs, in part, to develop a more complete database. FinCEN has not set a date for completion of this effort as its plans have not been finalized.

FinCEN officials told us that under the new rule, monitoring and compliance may be performed by its Office of Compliance, Office of Enforcement, and IRS' Fraud/BSA. However, even if it is able to develop a more complete database of MSBs, the degree to which IRS will monitor MSBs involved in issuing, selling, and redeeming stored value is an open question. For example, in March 2010, IRS told us that MSBs which provide stored value services generally have not been the target of compliance exams in recent years. IRS Fraud/BSA officials told us that most MSBs they examined for fiscal years 2007 through 2009 provided some other financial service (e.g. money transmission, check cashing, and issuing and selling traveler's checks) as their primary financial service, and may have conducted stored value transactions as an auxiliary financial service. IRS Fraud/BSA work plans during this period as well as for the current fiscal year (2010) excluded examination of MSBs whose primary financial service is stored value for the following two reasons: (1) most MSBs that were examined provided multiple financial services of which stored value may have been only one of them, and (2) the existing statutory requirements for entities that offer stored value products are minimal and IRS resource expenditures would be more beneficial in focusing on other MSBs.[114]

FinCEN's Efforts to Close Gaps in Anti-Money Laundering Regulations for Off-Shore Entities Has Made Progress, but More Work Remains

Combating the use of stored value by criminals involves not only efforts to implement anti-money laundering practices domestically, but also involves extending these efforts to international financial markets. Stored value issuers outside of the United States are generally not subject to FinCEN's anti-money laundering regulations, even though the stored value products they issue may be used in the United States or elsewhere in the world. Such devices can be used to load money from this country and download money in foreign countries through ATMs.

Prior to enactment of the Credit CARD Act, FinCEN had begun the process of proposing a new rule to address, among other things, off-shore MSBs that market their stored value products in the United States but the final rule is being delayed.[115] As of April 2010, agency officials told us its final rule related to off-shore MSBs will be delayed and issued at the time FinCEN issues the final rule addressing the requirements under the Credit CARD Act. This would allow for the provisions in both rules to be synchronized along with appropriate references because the two rules are closely related to one another.

Meanwhile, one way Treasury and FinCEN are addressing off-shore providers of stored value is through an intergovernmental entity called the Financial Action Task Force (FATF). FATF's purpose is to establish international standards and to develop and promote policies for combating money laundering and terrorist financing. In 2006, FATF issued a study[116] concluding that providers of new payment methods, such as stored value and mobile payments that are outside the jurisdiction of a given country, may pose additional risks of money laundering when (1) the distribution channel being used is the Internet, (2) there is no face-to-face contact with the customer, and (3) the new payment network operates through an open network that can be accessed in a high number of jurisdictions (e.g. ATMs worldwide). More recently, in its Strategic Plan (2008-2012) FinCEN recognized that to address the risk of cross-border transport and money laundering through the use of such devices calls for an approach that involves international cooperation with regulatory and law enforcement agencies outside of the United States. The degree to which FinCEN will succeed in gaining the cooperation of agencies outside of the United States in regulating stored value remains an open question. Officials at three of six law enforcement agencies we spoke with expressed concern about the risk of money laundering from off-shore MSBs.

According to Treasury officials we interviewed, the agency led the 2006 effort to disclose risks of money laundering related to off-shore MSBs that sell and issue stored value products and informed us that a new effort is currently under way to update the conditions and findings to see what more needs to be done to deter the use of such products for money laundering and terrorist financing activities. Treasury officials told us the updated report is being co-chaired by FATF representatives from Germany and the Netherlands with Treasury as a participating member. Although originally scheduled for June 2010, the revised issuance date for the updated report on new payment methods is October 2010.

FinCEN May Need to Evaluate Alternative Approaches to the Proposed Rule

In the NPRM, FinCEN has included a request for comments on the proposed rule, as well as 15 questions it asks stakeholders to comment on. For example, FinCEN's proposed rule exempts certain types of prepaid devices from anti-money laundering requirements. Specifically, the proposed rule exempts those devices that are (1) used to distribute payroll or benefits;[117] (2)

used to distribute government benefits; or (3) used for pre-tax flexible spending accounts for health care and dependent care expenses. The proposed rule also exempts programs offering closed system products that can only be used domestically as well as products that limit the maximum value and transactions to $1,000 or less at any given time.[118] As stated in the NPRM, FinCEN recognizes that some members of the law enforcement community have expressed concern about exempting prepaid access payroll programs from anti-money laundering requirements. To address concerns such as these, FinCEN has requested comments on methods for ensuring that the company and its employees are legitimate, and that the program is valid. FinCEN has also asked for comments on the $1,000 a day threshold as it may apply to transactions involving multiple MSBs. According to FinCEN, it will consider this matter and any comments that it receives. In doing so, when FinCEN reviews the comments it receives, it may need to evaluate alternatives to exempting such prepaid programs to address the risk of money laundering and the transport of such devices across the nation's borders to finance illegal activities. OMB Circular A-4 and Executive Order 12866, as amended, indicate that analysis of alternatives is a key component in assessing proposed rules.[119]

FinCEN Acknowledges that Outreach Will Help Ensure Industry Compliance With the New Rules

While the June 2010 NPRM proposes regulations that would require each "provider of prepaid access" to register with FinCEN and carry out anti-money laundering requirements related to prepaid access, the degree to which providers will register with FinCEN and carry out the proposed requirements remains an open question. FinCEN may face two challenges in this regard. First, while the proposed rule describes characteristics of MSBs that may qualify as a provider, entities in the prepaid access industry may not immediately know whether they are a provider without further clarification from FinCEN. This condition could lead to entities not registering as a provider when FinCEN intends that they follow the anti- money laundering requirements for such entities. Second, while sellers are exempt from registration requirements under the proposed rule, they are required to comply with certain anti-money laundering requirements. Not knowing whether the universe of providers and sellers is complete and accurate may hinder compliance efforts. As a result, FinCEN may face a higher risk of noncompliance without a program to educate industry about the rule and how to apply it.

In July 2010, FinCEN officials told us that they typically develop and conduct industry outreach, as resources allow, supporting the implementation of major new rulemakings. FinCEN officials explained that these outreach activities greatly assist covered industries in better understanding the new rules and how the new rules are to be applied. Because the prepaid access rulemaking is ongoing and FinCEN is awaiting feedback on its proposed regulations, preparations and planning for outreach to providers of prepaid access and other affected industry participants are in the initial phases, according to agency officials. Officials told us that FinCEN will continue its discussions with the Bank Secrecy Act Advisory Group and its Subcommittees to gain insight on how best to reach those affected by any final regulations. According to FinCEN, the level of effort associated with a major industry outreach effort of this kind will be significant.

CONCLUSIONS

Moving illegal proceeds across the border, whether in the form of bulk cash or stored value, represents a significant threat to national security. While CBP's outbound inspection effort has shown some early results, particularly in terms of bulk cash seized, the program's future is uncertain. If DHS continues to conduct outbound inspections, CBP faces important decisions regarding resources and processes for outbound inspections, and without all the necessary information, CBP may be unable to most effectively inform decisions on where scarce resources need to be applied. In addition, CBP could also improve its Outbound Enforcement Program by directing and ensuring ports of entry develop guidance that addresses officer safety. Also, by establishing performance measures related to program effectiveness, CBP could be better positioned to show the degree to which its efforts are stemming the flow of cash, weapons, and other goods that stem from criminal activities. While we recognize that this is a new program, without data and information to inform resource decisions, help ensure that officers are safe, and measure program effectiveness, CBP risks that the program could result in an inefficient use of resources, that officers will be endangered, and that Congress could not have the information it needs for its oversight efforts.

Even if efforts to reduce the flow of bulk cash into Mexico are successful, drug trafficking organizations and other criminal elements may shift their tactics and use other methods to smuggle illegal proceeds out of the United States, such as through the use of stored value. FinCEN is in the process of developing and issuing regulations related to the issuance of stored value, as required by the Credit CARD Act, but work remains and it is unclear when the agency will issue the final regulation. By developing a management plan with timelines for issuing final rules, FinCEN could be better positioned to manage its rulemaking efforts and to reduce the risk of cross-border smuggling and other illicit uses of stored value by drug trafficking organizations and others. Developing policies and procedures, such as for transaction testing for monitoring MSBs that issue, sell, and redeem stored value could help ensure that such MSBs carry out current and future anti-money laundering requirements.

RECOMMENDATIONS FOR EXECUTIVE ACTION

To strengthen CBP's implementation of the Outbound Enforcement Program as well as its planning efforts related to the program, we recommend that the Secretary of Homeland Security direct the Commissioner of Customs and Border Protection to take the following three actions:

- Collect cost and benefit data that would enable a cost/benefit analysis of the Outbound Enforcement Program to better inform decisions on where scarce resources should be applied. These data could include cost data on training and using currency canine for outbound operations as part of the Outbound Workload Staffing Model, cost estimates for equipping officers, installing technology to support outbound operations, assessments of infrastructure needs at port of entry outbound lanes, an estimate of the costs resulting from travelers waiting to be inspected, and information on quantifiable benefits, such as seizures, as well as non-quantifiable benefits resulting from outbound inspections.
- Direct and ensure that managers at land ports of entry develop policies and procedures that address officer safety, such as detailing how officers should conduct outbound inspections on a busy highway environment.
- Develop a performance measure that informs CBP management, Congress, and other stakeholders about the extent to which the Outbound Enforcement Program is effectively stemming the flow of bulk cash, weapons, and other goods that stem from criminal activities by working with other federal law enforcement agencies involved in

developing assessments on bulk cash and other illegal goods leaving the country.

To strengthen FinCEN's rulemaking process and to ensure IRS compliance examiners consistently apply the anti-money laundering requirements under the Credit CARD Act, we recommend that the Director of FinCEN take the following two actions:

- Update its written plan by describing, at a minimum, target dates for implementing all of the requirements under the Credit CARD Act to include FinCEN's overall strategy and risk mitigation plans and target dates for issuing notices of proposed rulemaking and final rules.
- Revise its guidance manual to include specific examination policies and procedures, including for transaction testing, for IRS examiners to follow at a MSB that issues, sells, and/or redeems stored value.

APPENDIX I. COSTS FOR OUTBOUND ENFORCEMENT PROGRAM (FISCAL YEARS 2008-2010)

Expense Item	Fiscal year 2008	Fiscal year 2009	Fiscal year 2010 (projected)
Headquarters/Mission support	42,708,955	50,782,988	68,335,263
Salaries and benefits	38,165,223	48,375,984	65,159,909
Overtime	3,980,533	4,918,598	5,546,535
Premium Pay[a]	2,571,585	3,089, 091	4,388,725
Supplies, Equipment, and Communication	499,796	545,259	798,514
Other non-labor[b]	294,204	326,590	390,586
Rent and facilities	289,173	312,252	426,470
Travel, training, and transportation	206,124	261,883	246,349
Total	**88,715,593**	**108,612,645**	**145,292,351**

Source: GAO analysis of CBP data.

Note: CBP conducted outbound operations before the Outbound Enforcement Program Office was created in March 2009.

[a] Holiday, Sunday, and night pay.

[b] Miscellaneous expenses.

APPENDIX II: GENERAL OVERVIEW OF THE FEDERAL RULEMAKING PROCESS

This appendix provides an overview of the steps in the rulemaking process for a significant regulatory action under Executive Order 12866, as amended, and the potential time involved for some of the steps.

Step 1: Agency (or agencies, if a joint rule) completes development of the notice of proposed rule making (NPRM), which includes the proposed rule and supplemental information.[120]

Step 2: Agency submits the draft NPRM and supporting materials, including any required cost-benefit analysis, to the Office of Management and Budget (OMB) for review.

Step 3: OMB reviews the draft NPRM and supporting materials and coordinates review of the proposed rule by any other agencies that may have an interest in it.

Step 4: OMB notifies the agency in writing of the results of its review, including any provisions requiring further consideration by the agency, within 90 calendar days after the date of submission to OMB.[121]

Step 5: OMB resolves disagreements or conflicts, if any, between or among agency heads or between OMB and any agency; if it cannot do so, such disagreements or conflicts are resolved by the President or by the Vice President acting at the request of the President.

Step 6: Once OMB notifies the agency that it has completed its review without any requests for further consideration, the agency reviews the NPRM and publishes it for public comment in the *Federal Register*.

Step 7: Agency is to give the public a meaningful opportunity to comment on the proposed rule, which generally means a comment period of not less than 60 days.

Step 8: Once the comment period has closed, the agency reviews the comments received, makes appropriate revisions to the proposed rule, and prepares a notice of the final rule, including supplemental information with responses to comments received.[122]

Step 9: Agency submits draft notice and final rule, including updated supporting materials or cost-benefit analysis, to OMB for review.

Step 10: OMB reviews the draft notice, final rule, and supporting materials; coordinates review by any other agencies that may have an interest in the rule; and notifies the agency of the results within 90 calendar days after the date of submission to OMB.[123]

Step 11: Once OMB notifies the agency that it has completed its review without any requests for further consideration, the agency reviews the rule one more time and generally publishes the final rule and supplemental information in the *Federal Register* at least 60 days before the new rule takes effect.

APPENDIX III. COMMENTS FROM THE DEPARTMENT OF HOMELAND SECURITY

U.S. Department of Homeland Security
Washington, DC 20528

Homeland Security

September 9, 2010

Richard M. Stana
Director, Homeland Security and Justice
441 G Street, NW
U.S. Government Accountability Office
Washington, DC 20548

Dear Mr. Stana:

RE: Response to Draft Report GAO-10-983, MOVING ILLEGAL PROCEEDS: Challenges Exist in the Federal Government's Effort to Stem Cross-Border Currency Smuggling

Thank you for the opportunity to review and comment on the Government Accountability Office's (GAO) draft report referenced above (Job Code 440800). The Department of Homeland Security (DHS), particularly U.S. Customs and Border Protection (CBP), concurs with the recommendations in the draft report and offers the following response.

Recommendation 1: Collect cost and benefit data that would enable a cost/benefit analysis of the OEP to better inform decisions on where scarce resources should be applied. These data could include cost data on training and using currency canine for outbound operations as part of the Outbound Workload Staffing Model, cost estimates for equipping officers, installing technology to support outbound operations, assessments of infrastructure needs at port of entry outbound lanes, an estimate of the costs resulting from travelers waiting to be inspected, and information on quantifiable benefits, such as seizures, as well as non-quantifiable benefits resulting from outbound inspections.

Response: Concur. CBP's Office of Field Operations (OFO), Outbound Enforcement Division (OED), is using a Project Integrator to identify cost estimates for Tier 1, Tier 2 and Tier 3 outbound land border solutions. OED is utilizing a project integrator that has begun collecting data such as infrastructure, tools and technology, canine, staffing, port volumes and hours of operation to further develop the cost/benefit analysis with a BorderWizard Tool.

OED is coordinating with the OFO—Offices of: Planning, Program Analysis and Evaluation (PPAE) and Mission Support (MS) to better identify quantifiable and non-quantifiable benefits. The collection and analysis of outbound data will greatly improve CBP's ability to conduct a cost/benefit analysis of the outbound program.

PPAE's Workload Staffing Model (WSM) does not compile and analyze cost data, as noted in the recommendation: "*These data could include cost data on training and using currency canine for outbound operations as part of the Outbound Workload Staffing Model.*" The

WSM focuses on specific work attributes instead of cost drivers. As the outbound operation develops these work attributes then the WSM can be enhanced to address the expected outbound mission and processes, including estimates of volumes, processing times, etc.

Also note that the WSM has been updated and some outbound operations modeling were recently integrated into the existing WSM. While the outbound operations modeling is not based on workload data drivers, the model integrates research from the OED as to how many Customs and Border Protection Officers (CBPOs) are needed and where they should be deployed if funding is provided. Furthermore, the WSM Program is continuously seeking to improve the model. As described above, the Outbound portion of the model can be enhanced to be a better predictor of the staffing investment required for the OED once the mission, scope, and the outbound program processes (or various options for these) are defined further.

Completion Date: May 30, 2011

Recommendation 2: Direct and ensure that managers at land ports of entry develop policies and procedures that address officer safety, such as detailing how officers should conduct outbound inspections on a busy highway environment.

Response: Concur. OED is updating the National Outbound Operations Policy Directive to include Section 5.6.1 "Directors of Field Operations (DFOs) will ensure that each Port Director has established an Officers' Safety Standard Operating Procedures (SOP) and implemented an on-the-job-training orientation program for outbound operations to ensure CBPOs are aware of the port's unique outbound safety hazards and challenges."

The issuance of national directives served to promote uniformity in CBP's border security mission. Because of the unique challenges identified at CBP's diverse ports of entry, the OED is unable to establish one standard national safety SOP, but will require that each Port Director develop a safety SOP based on the unique challenges at the port of entry.

Completion Date: January 31, 2011

Recommendation 3: Develop a performance measure that informs CBP management, Congress and other stakeholders about the extent to which the OED is effectively stemming the flow of bulk cash, weapons, and other goods that stem from criminal activities by working with other federal law enforcement agencies involved in developing assessments on bulk cash and other illegal goods leaving the country.

Response: Concur. OED and PPAE are currently working with the Department of Homeland Security's (DHS's) Program Analysis and Evaluation (PA&E) Office to develop appropriate Outbound/Exit performance measures that support the expansion of outbound activities and meet departmental and external reporting needs as part of a comprehensive PA&E performance measures improvement initiative in support of the requirements outlined in the DHS Quadrennial Homeland Security Review.

CBP currently conducts periodic, surge-type outbound operations which are limited in scope and do not cover the full range of outbound activity. OED and PA&E are working to develop effective performance measures that accurately assess the impact of conducting outbound operations given these limitations and the concurrent deterrence effect often observed with surge-type operations. CBP has no basis for developing a broad measure of the extent to

2

which OED is stemming the flow of bulk cash, weapons, and other goods from criminal activities.

To increase the effectiveness of outbound operations and our ability to assess the results of our efforts, CBP is coordinating enforcement activity with other federal law enforcement agencies to include DHS components, the Department of Justice and the White House, Office of National Drug Control Policy, to enhance CBP interdiction efforts. CBP will continue to identify trends in interdiction activities while focusing on areas identified in national threat assessments.

PPAE is investigating the implementation of a COMPEX-like random sampling process in the outbound environment that would provide statistically valid compliance results for outbound operations. This implementation is dependent on the required technology enablers, as outlined in the Land Border Outbound Solutions development plan, being in place prior to deployment.

Completion Date: September 30, 2011 (Implementation - PA&E measure improvement process)

Thank you for the opportunity to comment on this Draft Report and we look forward to working with you on future homeland security issues.

Sincerely,

Jerald E. Levine
Director
Departmental GAO/OIG Liaison Office

APPENDIX IV. COMMENTS FROM THE DEPARTMENT OF THE TREASURY

DEPARTMENT OF THE TREASURY
FINANCIAL CRIMES ENFORCEMENT NETWORK

DIRECTOR

September 3, 2010

Mr. Richard M. Stana
Director, Homeland Security and Justice
U.S. Government Accountability Office
441 G Street N.W.
Washington, D.C. 20515

Dear Mr. Stana:

We appreciate the review by the Government Accountability Office (GAO) of federal efforts to control the use of stored value and thank you for the opportunity to review and comment on the draft report entitled, *Moving Illegal Proceeds: Challenges Exist in the Federal Government's Effort to Stem Cross-Border Currency Smuggling.* As administrator of the Bank Secrecy Act (BSA), the Financial Crimes Enforcement Network (FinCEN) is responsible for effective, efficient, and consistent application of the BSA. FinCEN's proposed rulemaking for prepaid access products or services is intended to bring non-bank entities in the prepaid access sector under regulatory oversight that is more consistent with the obligations of other financial sectors subject to the BSA. However, as the report accurately notes, there are many challenges involved in establishing a new regulatory regime and ensuring compliance for an industry continually evolving with technology.

FinCEN works with a diverse range of stakeholders to administer the BSA, including financial industry regulators, law enforcement, and intelligence officials, as well as the industry members themselves. The diverse interests and needs of all stakeholders require careful thought and consideration when imposing new requirements to ensure that we obtain the right balance between financial transparency for law enforcement with the compliance obligations placed on industry. Thus, we appreciate GAO's recognition that federal rulemaking can be a lengthy process for significant regulatory actions, including those for prepaid access.

As noted in the June 2010 notice of proposed rulemaking for prepaid access, we anticipate issuing additional rulemaking to address all areas of potential vulnerability in the prepaid access sector. Although identifying target dates is particularly challenging when taking a phased approach to rulemaking, we agree that our existing plan should be updated accordingly. Additionally, when the initial rulemaking is finalized, we will proceed with our plan to update the Money Services Business examination manual and other related outreach efforts.

If you have any questions, please feel free to contact Jamal El-Hindi, Associate Director, Regulatory Policy and Programs Division, 202-354-6400.

Sincerely,

/s/

James H. Freis, Jr.

www.fincen.gov

End Notes

[1] Under 31 U.S.C. § 5332, bulk cash smuggling is defined as knowingly concealing and transporting or attempting to transport more than $10,000 in currency or monetary instruments into or out of the United States with the intent to evade the federal reporting requirements. Under 31 U.S.C. § 5316, a person or an agent or bailee of the person must file a report when the person, agent, or bailee knowingly transports, is about to transport, or has transported, monetary instruments of more than $10,000 at one time into or out of the United States.

[2] These figures were derived by multiplying the total quantity of Mexico-and Columbia-produced drugs available at the wholesale level in the United States by wholesale prices for those drugs. See U.S. Department of Justice, National Drug Intelligence Center, *2009 National Drug Threat Assessment* (Johnstown, Pa.: December 2008). Using a different method, NDIC estimated that at least $17 billion was smuggled into Mexico in bulk cash shipments alone over a 2-year period. NDIC based this estimate on a review of U.S. banknotes repatriated from Mexico. The estimate represents only U.S. currency returned to the United States not all U.S. currency that was smuggled to or through Mexico. This estimate is based on analysis of U.S. banknotes purchased by U.S. financial institutions from Mexican financial institutions from 2003 through 2004. See U.S. Department of Justice, National Drug Intelligence Center, *2010 National Drug Threat Assessment*, (Johnstown, Pa.: February 2010).

[3] U.S. Department of Justice, National Drug Intelligence Center, *2009 National Drug Threat Assessment* (Johnstown, Pa.: December 2008).

[4] Under 31 C.F.R. § 103.11(vv), stored value is defined as funds or monetary value represented in digital electronics format (whether or not specifically encrypted) and stored or capable of storage on electronic media in such a way as to be retrievable and transferable electronically.

[5] Money Laundering Threat Assessment Working Group, *U.S. Money Laundering Threat Assessment* (December 2005).

[6] Ports of entry are government-designated locations where CBP inspects persons and goods to determine whether they may be lawfully admitted or entered into the country. A land port of entry may have more than one border crossing where CBP inspections occur.

[7] FinCEN is within the Office of Terrorism and Financial Intelligence. This office aims to prevent terrorism and promote the nation's security through strengthened international financial systems.

[8] National Drug Intelligence Center, *2009 National Drug Threat Assessment* (Johnstown, Pa., December 2008) and National Drug Intelligence Center, *2010 National Drug Threat Assessment* (Johnstown, Pa., February 2010).

[9] National Drug Intelligence Center, *Reassessing Southwest Border Bulk Cash Smuggling: Consolidation Points as Trafficker Vulnerabilities*, (Johnstown, Pa., March 2008).

[10] Immigration and Customs Enforcement, *Mexico Bulk Currency Study* (Washington D.C.: November 2009).

[11] GAO, *Standards for Internal Control in the Federal Government*, GAO/AIMD-00-21.3.1 (Washington, D.C.: November 1999). These standards, issued pursuant to the requirements of the Federal Managers' Financial Integrity Act of 1982 (FMFIA), provide the overall framework for establishing and maintaining internal control in the federal government. Also pursuant to FMFIA, the Office of Management and Budget (OMB) issued Circular A123, revised December 21, 2004, to provide the specific requirements for assessing the reporting on internal controls. Internal control standards and the definition of internal control in OMB Circular A-123 are based on GAO's *Standards for Internal Control in the Federal Government*.

[12] Under 31 C.F.R. § 103.11 (uu) (1)-(6), MSBs are generally defined as any of the following (1) currency dealer or exchanger, (2) check casher, (3) issuer of traveler's checks, money orders, or stored value, (4) seller or redeemer of traveler's checks, money orders, or stored value, (5) money transmitter, and (6) the U.S. Post Office. Banks and persons registered with and regulated or examined by, the Securities and Exchange Commission or the Commodity Futures Trading Commission have been excluded from the definition of an MSB.

[13] The margin of error for percentages for the sample of 400 reports is plus or minus 5 percentage points or less at the 95 percent level of statistical confidence.

[14] Pub. L. No. 111-24, 123 Stat. 1734 (2009).

[15] Amendments to the Bank Secrecy Act Regulations-Definitions and other Regulations Relating to Prepaid Access, 75 Fed. Reg. 36589 (proposed June 28, 2010).

[16] GAO/AIMD-00-21.3. 1.

[17] CBP may refer criminals or individuals who violate laws and regulations to ICE for further investigation.

[18] Office of National Drug Control Policy, *Southwest Border Counternarcotics Strategy* (Washington D.C.: June 2009).

[19] CBP operates 25 land ports of entry along the southwest border and 81 land ports of entry along the Northern border. Some land ports may contain multiple crossings where travelers can exit the country.

[20] When interviewing travelers who seek to enter or return to the United States, the Immigration and Nationality Act (See 8 U.S.C. § 1225(a)) and implementing regulations (See 8 C.F.R. § 235. 1(a), (b), (f)(1)) and CBP policies and procedures for traveler inspections at all ports of entry require officers to establish, at a minimum, the nationality of individuals and whether they are eligible to enter the country. To do so, CBP officers review documents and databases, and ask a series of questions to establish whether the traveler is a U.S. citizen or alien, and if an alien, whether the person meets the criteria for admission into the country. In general, nonimmigrant aliens arriving at land and air ports of entry must present a valid, unexpired passport as well as, depending on the country of origin and intended length of stay in the United States, a valid, unexpired visa issued by a U.S. embassy or consulate for entry into the country.

[21] 31 U.S.C. § 5316; 31 C.F.R. § 103.23. Generally, each person who physically transports, mails, or ships, or causes to be physically transported, mailed, or shipped currency or other monetary instruments in an aggregate amount exceeding $10,000 at one time from the United States to any place outside the United States or into the United States from any place outside the United States must make a report of transportation of currency or monetary instruments.

[22] 31 U.S.C. § 5316; 31 C.F.R. § 103.23. For travelers who carry or individuals who ship, mail, or receive more than $10,000 in currency or other monetary instruments, such as traveler's checks or money orders, into or out of the U.S., CBP requires them to fill out a form called the Report of International Transportation of Currency or Monetary Instruments. When travelers fail to file a form, file a form with material omission, or misstatement, or file a false or fraudulent form, they are subject to civil and criminal penalties, including under certain circumstances a fine of not more the $500,000 or imprisonment of not more than 10 years, or both. In addition, the currency or monetary instrument may be subject to seizure and forfeiture.

[23] Under 31 C.F.R. § 103.11(u), monetary instruments include (i) currency; (ii) travelers' checks in any form; (iii) all negotiable instruments (including personal checks, business checks, official bank checks, cashier's checks, third-party checks, promissory notes (as that term is defined in the Uniform Commercial Code), and money orders) that are either in bearer form, endorsed without restriction, made out to a fictitious payee for the purposes of the international transportation reporting requirement or otherwise in such form that title thereto passes upon delivery; (iv) incomplete instruments (including personal checks, business

checks, official bank checks, cashier's checks, third-party checks, promissory notes (as that term is defined in the Uniform Commercial Code), and money orders) signed but with the payee's name omitted; and (v) securities or stock in bearer form or otherwise in such form that title thereto passes upon delivery. Monetary instruments do not include warehouse receipts or bills of lading.

[24] 31 U.S.C. § 5332.

[25] According to the World Bank, almost half the world's population owns a cell phone and it estimates that 1.4 billion people will use cell phones to remit money domestically and across borders by 2015. See The World Bank, *Integrity in Mobile Phone Financial Services: Measures for Mitigating Risks from Money Laundering and Terrorist Financing,* (Washington D.C.: 2008). According to the Financial Action Task Force, an organization whose purpose is to establish international standards and to develop and promote policies for combating money laundering and terrorist financing, a cell phone can be used as a payment system access device to authorize the deduction of value from a prepaid account.

[26] Bank Secrecy Act, titles I and II of Pub. L. No. 9 1-508, 84 Stat. 1114 (1970) (codified as amended in 12 U.S.C. §§ 1829b, 1951-1959; 31 U.S.C. §§ 5311-5332).

[27] The Secretary of the Treasury has the authority to administer the BSA and its implementing regulations. This authority has been delegated by the Secretary to the Director of FinCEN.

[28] 31 U.S.C. §§ 5318, 5313.

[29] The Director of FinCEN reports to the Under Secretary, Office of Terrorism and Financial Intelligence.

[30] Among other things, the support FinCEN provides to domestic law enforcement agencies, in their efforts to investigate and prosecute financial crimes, includes a variety of services and products such as providing access to BSA data, responding to requests from law enforcement agencies for information pertaining to specific investigations, and producing analytic products covering a range of issues related to financial crimes. FinCEN also works with law enforcement at the state and local level as well as collaborates with international counterparts in other countries to facilitate sharing of financial information between domestic and international law enforcement agencies. For more information, see GAO, *Anti-Money Laundering: Improved Communication Could Enhance the Support FinCEN Provides to Law Enforcement*, GAO-10-141, (Washington D.C.: December 14, 2009).

[31]See 31 C.F.R. § 103.11(uu).

[32]In 2005, KPMG, a consulting firm, attempted to estimate the transaction volume of MSBs nationwide for FinCEN by surveying 24,000 MSBs. The study estimated that MSBs accounted for about $300 billion in annual transaction volume. This estimate excluded the U.S. Postal Service, an entity that falls under the definition of MSB because it offers money order services. However, because the survey obtained an 8 percent response rate the large percentage of nonresponses may have affected the survey results. See KPMG, LLP Economic and Valuation Services, *2005 Money Services Business Industry Survey Study* (Washington D.C.: September 2005).

[33] See 31 C.F.R. § 103.11(vv).

[34] Dove Consulting, *The Electronics Payments Study, A Survey of Electronic Payments for the 2007 Federal Reserve Payments Study*, (Boston, Ma.: March 2008). The scope of the study involved collecting data on electronic payments made in the United States in 2006. According to the study, prepaid card adoption has grown and is emerging as a potentially important component of the electronic payments mix, such as credit cards and debit cards.

[35] Dove Consulting, The Electronics Payments Study, A Survey of Electronic Payments for the 2007 Federal Reserve Payments Study (Boston, Ma.: March 2008).

[36] Money Laundering Threat Assessment Working Group, *2005 U.S. Money Laundering Threat Assessment*, (December 2005).

[37] The World Bank, *Integrity in Mobile Phone Financial Services: Measures for Mitigating Risks from Money Laundering and Terrorist Financing* (Washington D.C.: 2008).

[38] Prior to September 11, 2001, the former U.S. Customs Service conducted outbound inspections in a routine fashion using permanent outbound teams. After this date, port directors had the discretion to continue outbound operations, but the Customs Service shifted its focus to inbound inspections to prevent terrorists from entering the country. During this time, only two ports of entry continued to conduct outbound operations in a routine fashion—Hidalgo, Texas and Laredo, Texas. In 2003, the U.S. Customs Service was merged with components of the U.S. Immigration and Naturalization Service and the Animal and Plant Health Inspection Service to form Customs and Border Protection. The Outbound Enforcement Program was reestablished, under CBP, on March 12, 2009, when the Secretary of Homeland Security called on CBP to stem the flow of cash and weapons that were being taken into Mexico through land ports of entry.

[39] While this report focuses on currency smuggling, we previously issued a report on firearms trafficking in June 2009, entitled *Firearms Trafficking: U.S. Efforts to Combat Arms Trafficking to Mexico Face Planning and Coordination Challenges,* GAO-09-709 (Washington, D.C.: June 2009).

[40] According to CBP, it conducted 4,217,883 outbound interviews and 3,002,716 outbound inspections from March 12, 2009 through July 13, 2010. An interview consists of the officer asking the traveler whether they (1) intend to leave the country, (2) are carrying more than $10,000 in cash, checks, money orders, or any other type of monetary instrument, and (3) are transporting any weapons or ammunitions out of the country. An inspection involves the searching of a vehicle, passenger, or pedestrian. For example, an inspection might involve inspecting the content of the vehicle, such as opening a trunk of a car and examining the vehicle for hidden compartments where cash may be concealed.

[41] Among other items, the targeting module discusses how to research possible links to terrorist and criminal organizations. The inspecting module covers questioning for outbound inspections and the physical inspection of vehicles and individuals. The processing module instructs officers on how to seize vehicles, currency, and other monetary instruments.

[42] There are 144 training slots available for fiscal year 2010.

[43] DHS and the Department of State's effort to specify acceptable documents and implement document requirements at air, land, and sea ports of entry is called the Western Hemisphere Travel Initiative.

[44] During this time, CBP seized about $40.0 million in bulk cash leaving the country at ports of entry on the southwest border. CBP also seized about $1.2 million in bulk cash leaving the country at ports of entry on the Northern border. On the Northern border, outbound inspections are conducted at the discretion of the Port Director. CBP officials report that unlike seizures at the southwest border, outbound seizures along the Northern border are primarily drugs flowing out of the United States into Canada, specifically cocaine. The cocaine is generally purchased in the Los Angeles area after being shipped through Mexico and is then transported to Canada, where it can be sold at a higher price.

[45] This calculation assumes the start of the Outbound Enforcement Program to be March 1, 2009. During the first year of the program, CBP seized $34.0 million in outbound cash at land ports of entry along the southwest and Northern borders as compared to $16.8 million in the year leading up to the program.

[46] In addition to CBP, other law enforcement agencies also seize bulk cash leaving the country. For example, in fiscal year 2009, ICE had more than 1,200 seizures totaling over $122 million.

[47] Along the Northern border, 9 of the 81 ports of entry also had at least one seizure while conducting outbound operations.

[48] Supplemental Appropriations Act, 2009, Pub. L. No. 111-32, 123 Stat. 1859, 1881.

[49] The three ports of entry did not have currency canines assigned to their locations.

[50] Our investigators used shredded cash so that there would not be a risk that real cash would be confiscated by CBP or Mexican officials. The shredded cash represented 3,000 bills, or about $60,000, if the cash were in $20 denominations.

[51] OMB, *Circular Number A-94* (Oct. 29, 1992).

[52] DHS, *Cost-Benefit Analysis Guidebook* (2006).

[53] Office of National Drug Control Policy, *National Southwest Border Counternarcotics Strategy* (Washington D.C.: June 2009).

[54] The Treasury Forfeiture Fund is derived from the forfeited assets of criminal enterprises. The fund is a "special receipt account" i.e., a resource account that provides funding to the participating law enforcement agencies to enhance their capabilities to conduct successful investigations and forfeitures.

[55] As we reported in July 2010, longer wait times at the border represent an increase in the cost of travel, which may lead people to make fewer trips. Conversely, shorter wait times represent a decrease in the cost of travel which may lead people to make more trips. Such delays can result in additional expenses for industry and consumers, stemming from increased carrier costs, inventory costs, labor costs, problems with inventory, and resulting reduction in trade and output. See GAO, *Border Security: CBP Lacks the Data Needed to Assess the FAST Program at U.S. Northern Border Ports,* GAO-10-694 (Washington D.C.: July 19, 2010).

[56] GAO-10-694.

[57] OMB, *Circular Number A-94*, (Oct. 29, 1992).

[58] GAO/AIMD-00.21.3. 1.

[59] The other nine steps that the Outbound Enforcement Program plans to take include (1) create an effective headquarters outbound team, (2) obtain an adequate budget for outbound activities, (3) evaluate and update the Office of Field Operations' outbound policies, (4) revise current Office of Field Operations' procedures to ensure the facilitation of legitimate trade and travelers, (5) update the *Federal Register's* outbound regulations to address current vulnerabilities, (6) improve CBP automated systems to track and target export shipments, (7) provide outbound training for CBP officers, embedded stakeholders, and state and local law enforcement officials, (8) increase collaboration with other governmental agencies and international partners and (9) improve outbound facilities.

[60] GAO, *Managing for Results: Enhancing Agency Use of Performance Information for Management Decision Making*, GAO-05-927 (Washington D.C.: Sept. 9, 2005).

[61] GAO/AIMD-00.21.3. 1.

[62] U.S. Department of Justice, National Drug Intelligence Center, *Reassessing Southwest Border Bulk Cash Smuggling: Consolidation Points as Trafficker Vulnerabilities*, (March 2008).

[63] Immigration and Customs Enforcement, *Mexico Bulk Currency Study: A Project Conducted by the Homeland Security Institute in Collaboration with U.S. Immigration and Customs Enforcement and the DHS Office of Counternarcotics Enforcement*, (Washington D.C.: Nov. 2009).

[64] The ICE Bulk Cash Smuggling Center's goal is to provide assistance to federal, state, local and foreign law enforcement authorities that combat bulk cash smuggling by providing intelligence, investigative support, and expertise in the transportation and smuggling of bulk cash.

[65] Stored value is the focus of this report. However, other methods exist for transporting proceeds from illegal activities across the nation's borders. For example, in addition to stored value, the 2005 United States Money Laundering Threat Assessment discusses the risk of money laundering through trade-based schemes, such as the Black Market Peso Exchange, and the use of shell companies.

[66] 31 U.S.C. § 5311.

[67] 31 U.S.C. § 5316; 31 C.F.R. § 103.23.

[68] "Issuer of stored value" and "seller or redeemer of stored value" are the current terms used to define the stored value industry under the Bank Secrecy Act regulations. FinCEN has proposed that these terms be changed. The proposed changes are discussed later in this report.

[69] 31 C.F.R. § 103.22.

[70] Some MSBs that offer stored value products may be subject to BSA regulations if that MSB also offers other financial services. For example, a MSB that operates as a money transmitter and also offers stored value products is required to register with Treasury in its capacity as a money transmitter. However, this MSB would be exempt from filing reports on suspicious transactions involving solely stored value. We explain the exemptions in more detail later in the report.

[71] Amendment to the Bank Secrecy Act Regulations-Definitions and Other Regulations Relating to Money Services Businesses, 74 Fed. Reg. 22129, 22136 (proposed May 12, 2009). See also Amendment to the Bank Secrecy Act Regulations-Definitions Relating to, and Registration of, Money Services Businesses, 64 Fed. Reg. 45438 (proposed Aug. 20, 1999).

[72] Department of the Treasury, Semiannual Regulatory Agenda, 75 Fed. Reg. 21868, 21869 (April 26, 2010).

[73] 31 U.S.C. § 5330; 31 C.F.R. § 103.41.

[74] Pub. L. No. 103-325 § 408(a)(2), 108 Stat. 2160, 2249-52.

[75] The registration requirements of 31 C.F.R. § 103.41 do not apply to the U.S. Postal Service, to agencies of the United States, of any State, or of any political subdivision of a State, a person that is a MSB solely because that person serves as an agent of another MSB, or to a person to the extent that the person is an issuer, seller, or redeemer of stored value.

[76] U.S. Departments of Treasury, Justice, and Homeland Security, *2007 National Money Laundering Strategy*, (Washington, D.C.: May 2007).

[77] Under 31 C.F.R. § 103.41, a person that is a MSB solely because that person serves as an agent of another MSB is not required to register.

[78] A 2005 study by KPMG attempted to estimate the total number of MSBs operating nationwide. The study estimated the number to be approximately 203,000. This estimate excludes the U.S Postal Service, an entity that falls under the definition of MSB because it offers money order services. However, because the survey obtained an 8 percent response rate, the large percentage of non-responses may have affected the survey results. See KPMG, LLP Economic and Valuation Services, 2005 Money Services Business Industry Survey Study, (Washington D.C.: September 2005).

[79] For example, in 2007, the Network Branded Prepaid Card Association released a set of anti-money laundering best practices for issuers of network-branded prepaid cards. These best practices included developing and implementing a customer identification program, particularly for reloadable cards that can be used to access cash.

[80] There is not a specific regulation on customer identification programs for MSBs. However, generally, financial institutions, including MSBs, are required to file currency transaction reports (CTR) for each deposit, withdrawal, exchange of currency or other payment or transfer, by, through, or to the financial institution which involves a transaction in currency of more than $10,000. 31 C.F.R. § 103.22. Before concluding any transaction with respect to which a CTR is required, a financial institution is required to verify and record the name and address of the individual presenting a transaction, as well as record the identity, account number, and the Social Security or taxpayer identification number, if any, of any person or entity on whose behalf such transaction is to be effected. 31 C.F.R. § 103.28.

[81] Treasury Cash Equivalent Working Group, *Prepaid Cards Primer and Threat Assessment* (2005).

[82] The USA PATRIOT Act of 2001, Pub. L. No. 107-56, 115 Stat. 272 (Oct. 26, 2001), expanded SAR reporting requirements to include nondepository institutions. However, under 31 C.F.R. § 103.20(a)(5), money services businesses are not required to file suspicious activity reports for transactions that involve solely the issuance, or facilitation of the transfer of stored value, or the issuance, sale, or redemption of stored value.

[83] Under 31 C.F.R. § 103.18, which discusses the filing of suspicious activity reports by banks, there is no exemption for stored value transactions.

[84] For transactions other than stored value, MSBs are generally required to file a suspicious activity report when a transaction is conducted or attempted by, at, or through a MSB,

involves or aggregates funds or other assets of at least $2,000, and the MSB knows, suspects, or has reason to suspect that the transactions or pattern of transactions: involves funds derived from illegal activities or is intended or conducted in order to hide or disguise funds or assets derived from illegal activity as part of a plan to violate or evade any federal law, regulation or reporting requirement under federal law or regulation; are designed to evade BSA requirements or other financial reporting requirements; have no business or apparent lawful purpose; or involve the use of the MSB to facilitate criminal activity.

[85] For more information, see GAO, *Bank Secrecy Act: Suspicious Activity Report Use Is Increasing, but FinCEN Needs to Further Develop and Document Its Form Revision Process*, GAO-09-226 (Washington, D.C.: Feb. 27, 2009).

[86] Of the 471 SARs filed that were associated with stored value cards, 137 were filed by depository institutions, 331 were filed by money services businesses, and 3 were filed by broker/dealers. Of note, a single MSB filed 188 of the 331 MSB forms identified.

[87] Structuring is when a person, acting alone, or in conjunction with, or on behalf of, other persons, conducts or attempts to conduct one or more transactions in currency, in any amount, at one or more financial institutions, on one or more days, in any manner, for the purpose of evading certain reporting requirements.

[88] U.S. Immigration and Customs Enforcement, *United States of America–Mexico: BiNational Criminal Proceeds Study* (Washington, D.C., June 2010).

[89] Of note, SARs do not necessarily represent known criminal activities, but rather suspicions. In many cases, the activity described in these SARs could be legitimate. Stored value products serve a legitimate purpose in serving the estimated 75 million individuals in the United States who do not have access to bank accounts.

[90] One law enforcement agency with whom we spoke did not express a concern about the lack of a cross-border reporting requirement for stored value. Another law enforcement agency with whom we spoke had no comment.

[91] Pub. L. No. 111-24, 123 Stat. 1734 (2009).

[92] Under 31 U.S.C. § 5316, a person or an agent or bailee of the person must file a report when the person, agent, or bailee knowingly transports, is about to transport, or has transported, monetary instruments of more than $10,000 at one time into or out of the United States.

[93] U nder the Credit CARD Act, the regulations were to be issued in final form no later than 270 days after the date of enactment of the act. The deadline for issuing regulations in final form was on February 16, 2010.

[94] Generally, the Administrative Procedure Act (APA) is the principal law governing how agencies make rules. The APA prescribes uniform standards for rule-making and most federal rules are promulgated using the APA-established informal rule-making process, also known as “notice and comment” rule-making. Generally, a notice of proposed rule-making (NPRM) is published in the *Federal Register* announcing an agency’s intent to promulgate a rule to the public. The APA requires that the NPRM include a statement of the time, place, and nature of the public rule-making proceedings, reference to the legal authority under which the rule is proposed, and the terms or substance of the proposed rule or a description of the subjects and issues involved. The NPRM also generally includes the timing and manner in which the public may comment on the proposed rule. Executive Order 12866, as amended, states that most rule-makings should include a comment period of 60 days, and most agencies do provide a 60-day or longer comment period for complex or controversial rules. After issuance of the NPRM, agencies are generally required to place public comments as well as other supporting materials in a rule-making docket which must be available for public inspection.

[95] See appendix II for a more detailed description of the steps and potential time frames involved in the rule-making process.

[96] FinCEN proposes to define “prepaid access” as an electronic device or vehicle, such as a card, plate, code, number, electronic serial number, mobile identification number, personal identification number, or other instrument that provides a portal to funds or the value of

funds that have been paid in advance and can be retrievable and transferable at some point in the future.

97 GAO, *Anti-Money Laundering: Improved Communication Could Enhance the Support FinCEN Provides to Law Enforcement*, GAO-10-141 (Washington, D.C.: Dec. 14, 2009).

98 Amendment to the Bank Secrecy Act Regulations-Definitions and Other Regulations Relating to Money Services Businesses, 74 Fed. Reg. 22129 (proposed May 12, 2009).

99 FinCEN proposes to define a "provider of prepaid access" as the person with principal oversight and control over one or more prepaid programs. Which person exercises "principal oversight and control" is a matter of facts and circumstances, but FinCEN considers the following activities to indicate "principal oversight and control:" (1) organizing the prepaid program; (2) setting the terms and conditions and determining that the terms have not been exceeded; (3) determining the other businesses that will participate in the transaction chain underlying the prepaid access which may include the issuing bank, the payment processor, or the distributor; (4) controlling or directing the appropriate party to initiate, freeze, or terminate prepaid access; and (5) engaging in activity that demonstrates oversight and control of transactions. FinCEN estimates that there are 700 entities that fall under its definition of provider. It also estimates that 93 percent, or about 650 entities, fall under the definition of a small business, or businesses with less than 7 million dollars in gross revenue.

100 FinCEN proposes to define "seller of prepaid access" as any person who receives funds or the value of funds in exchange for providing prepaid access as part of a prepaid program directly to the person that provided the funds or value, or to a third party as directed by that person. According to the NPRM, the seller of prepaid access is the party with the most face-to-face purchaser contact and becomes a valuable resource for capturing information at the point of sale. According to FinCEN, typically, the seller is a general-purpose retailer, engaged in a full spectrum product line through a business entity such as a pharmacy, convenience store, supermarket, discount store or any of a number of others. FinCEN estimates that there are about 70,000 sellers of stored value or prepaid access, as defined in its proposed rule and that a substantial number are small businesses.

101 The proposed rule would require prepaid providers and sellers to report on transactions of $2,000 or more which they determine to be suspicious.

102 Project Management Institute, *A Guide to the Project Management Body of Knowledge (PMBOK Guide)*, 4th ed. (Newton Square, Pa.: 2008).

103 The four federal agencies included in our study were (1) the Department Transportation's Federal Aviation Administration and National Highway Traffic Safety Administration, (2) the Environmental Protection Agency's Office of Air and Radiation and Office of Water, (3) the Food and Drug Administration's Center for Drug Evaluation and Research and Center for Food Safety and Applied Nutrition, and (4) the Securities and Exchange Commission's Division of Corporation Finance and Division of Investment Management.

104 GAO, *Federal Rule-making: Improvements Needed to Monitoring and Evaluation of Rules Development as Well as to the Transparency of OMB Regulatory Reviews*, GAO-09-205 (Washington, D.C.: Apr. 20, 2009).

105 FinCEN's *Bank Secrecy Act/Anti-Money Laundering Examination Manual For Money Services Businesses* was published on December 9, 2008. It provides guidance to examiners for carrying out MSB compliance examinations. An effective compliance program requires sound risk management; therefore, the manual also provides guidance on identifying and controlling risks associated with money laundering and terrorist financing. The manual contains an overview of compliance program requirements, risk and risk management expectations, industry sound practices, and examination procedures.

106 GAO/AIMD-00-21.3.1.

107 FinCEN has taken a number of steps to improve the overall quality and value of BSA data, such as SARs. For example, in fiscal year 2007, FinCEN established a Data Management Council as part of a broader BSA data management initiative. The Council consists of

approximately 35 representatives from FinCEN, law enforcement, regulatory agencies, and the IRS, and serves to ensure that internal and external data users have a clear means of jointly establishing priorities related to data management, among other roles. Additionally, in May 2008, FinCEN developed a new management process for revising BSA forms, such as the SAR form, under the auspices of its Data Management Council. The goals of this process, among others, are to improve communication between stakeholders involved in the BSA form revision process and to improve the implementation of revisions by FinCEN and other agencies.

[108] The narrative section of the form asks the financial institution filing the report to provide a chronological and complete account of the activity or possible violation of law, including what is unusual, irregular, or suspicious about the transaction.

[109] GAO worked with FinCEN staff to identify the search terms used. The terms decided on included: "stored value," "store value," "prepaid card," "prepaid debit," "prepaid credit," or "gift card." FinCEN searched its database and provided us with 13,327 SARs filed by Depository Institutions or Money Services Businesses for fiscal year 2009 and October through April in fiscal year 2010 containing narratives with at least one of the terms. We randomly selected and reviewed 100 SARS in each of the following categories: (1) SARs filed by depository institutions in fiscal year 2009; (2) SARs filed by depository institutions from October through April in fiscal year 2010; (3) SARs filed by money service businesses in fiscal year 2009; and (4) SARs filed by money service businesses from October through April in fiscal year 2010. First, an analyst reviewed the narrative and made a determination as to whether the report pertained to stored value. A second analyst reviewed this determination and the associated report for accuracy. All statistical samples are subject to sampling error; that is, the extent to which the sample results differ from what would have been obtained if the whole population had been observed. Measures of sampling error are defined by two elements, the width of the confidence intervals around the estimate (sometimes called the precision of the estimate) and the confidence level at which the intervals are computed. Because we followed a probability procedure based on random selections, our sample is only one of a large number of samples that we might have drawn. As each sample could have provided different estimates, we express our confidence in the precision of our particular sample's results as a 95 percent confidence interval (e.g., plus or minus 5 percentage points). This is the interval that would contain the actual population value for 95 percent of the samples we could have drawn. As a result, we are 95 percent confident that each of the confidence intervals based on the review of the files in this sample includes the true values in the population. The margin of error for estimated percentages for the combined sample of 400 SARs is plus or minus 5 percentage points or less at the 95 percent level of statistical confidence.

[110] The MSB population can range from large sophisticated chains with interstate operations that focus on providing a range of financial services such as check cashing and money transmission to small one-owner storefront operations that provide a few financial services, such as stored value cards as an auxiliary service to their primary retail store operations.

[111] Department of the Treasury, Office of the Inspector General, *Bank Secrecy Act: Major Challenges Faced by FinCEN in Its Program to Register Money Services Businesses*, OIG-05-050 (Washington, D.C.: Sept. 27, 2005).

[112] GAO, *Bank Secrecy Act: FinCEN and IRS Need to Improve and Better Coordinate Compliance and Data Management Efforts*, GAO-07-212 (Washington, D.C.: Dec. 15, 2006). In response to a recommendation cited in this report, IRS tried to determine whether its Small Business/Self-Employed Division taxpayer data base could be used to facilitate the identification of MSBs using a standard profile. However, IRS was unable to do so in part because it could not readily distinguish MSBs from non-MSBs in tax return data. In developing its methodology, IRS found that it could match taxpayer identification numbers for known MSBs from the NBFI to tax return data and create a profile of known MSBs. However, when developing a method for matching the MSB profile to the entire tax return

database, IRS found there were not any variables that could be used to distinguish MSBs from non-MSBs. In conjunction with this effort, IRS began another project to determine if outside data sources could be used to identify previously unknown MSBs using information compiled by a private data source. As potential MSBs are identified using these data, IRS sends correspondence to these entities and then examines them to determine whether any were a previously unidentified MSB. IRS has also acquired a second data source containing potential MSBs from a private firm which it also uses to identify such businesses.

113 U.S. Departments of Treasury, Justice, and Homeland Security, *2007 National Money Laundering Strategy* (Washington, D.C.: May 2007).

114 Although IRS Fraud/BSA work plans did not include MSBs having a primary financial service of stored value, officials told us the examiners classified some MSBs (a fraction of one percent) as having stored value as their primary financial service based on completed IRS Fraud/BSA examinations.

115 See Amendment to the Bank Secrecy Act Regulations—Definitions and Other Regulations Relating to Money Services Business, Notice of Proposed Rulemaking, 74 Fed. Reg. 22129, 22133-22134 (proposed May 12, 2009).

116 FATF – GAFI, *Financial Action Task Force: Report on New Payment Methods* (Paris, France: Oct. 13, 2006).

117 According to the NPRM, this exemption applies only when the employer (or appropriately designated third parties), and not the employee, can add to the funds to which the payroll card or other such electronic device provides access.

118 Specifically, the proposed rules exempt prepaid programs where the maximum dollar value is clearly visible on the product and the following conditions are met: (1) at the point of initial load, the load limit cannot exceed $1,000; (2) may not exceed $1,000 maximum aggregate value (such as through multiple transfers of value to a single prepaid access product) that can be associated with the prepaid access at any given time; and (3) on any given day, no more than $1,000 can be withdrawn with the use of the prepaid access.

119 The June 2010 NPRM states that "[T]his proposed rule is a significant regulatory action and has been reviewed by the Office of Management and Budget in accordance with Executive Order 12866." OMB Circular A-4 provides guidance on the development of regulatory impact analysis as required under Section 6(a)(3)(C) of Executive Order 12866, as amended.

120 An agency may also begin this process with an advance notice of proposed rule making that seeks comments and suggestions from the public on the potential content of a forthcoming NPRM, but this step is not required by law or executive order in most cases.

121 Executive Order 12866, as amended, provides that, for rules governed by a statutory deadline, the agency shall, to the extent practicable, schedule rulemaking proceedings so as to permit sufficient time for OMB review. It also provides that when an agency is obligated by law to act more quickly than normal review procedures allow, the agency shall comply with the requirements to submit the proposed rule and required supporting materials to OMB, "to the extent practicable."

122 If the final rule is materially different from the proposed rule, possibly because of new issues raised or other important legal or substantive developments during the comment period, an agency may decide to publish it as a proposed rule instead with a second comment period. This approach helps the agency provide sufficient notice and opportunity for public comment on how the rule addresses the new issues or developments, but it delays implementation of the final rule.

123 This time period is reduced to 45 days if OMB has previously reviewed the rule and supporting information and there has been no material change in the facts and circumstances upon which the rule is based.

In: Dirty Money
Editor: Donna P. Richards

ISBN: 978-1-61324-663-4

Chapter 2

Senate Caucus on International Narcotics Control Holds Hearing on Money Laundering and Bulk Cash Smuggling Across the Southwest Border

Washington, DC – U.S. Senators Dianne Feinstein (D-Calif.) and Chuck Grassley (R-Iowa), co-chairs of the Senate Caucus on International Narcotics Control, held a hearing today on Money Laundering and Bulk Cash Smuggling across the Southwest Border.

Following is the text of Senator Feinstein's prepared opening remarks:

We are here today because Mexico's brutal drug trafficking organizations are fueled by money that illegally transits from the United States to Mexico, much of it across our Southwest border.

Violence in Mexico has reached unprecedented levels. Since the start of Mexican President Felipe Calderón's administration in December 2006, over 34,000 people have died in drug-related killings in Mexico. The killings reached their highest level in 2010, jumping by almost 60 percent to 15,273 deaths from 9,616 the previous year.

I believe that the United States has a responsibility to curb the illegal flow of money into Mexico. Without reducing this illicit transit, it will be difficult to make significant progress in dismantling Mexican drug trafficking organizations. My hope is that today's hearing will push us all to do a better job in cutting off money destined for Mexico's violent drug traffickers.

According to the National Drug Intelligence Center, Mexican and Colombian drug trafficking organizations "annually generate, remove and launder between $18 billion and $39 billion in wholesale distribution proceeds," much of it across the Southwest border.

Millions of dollars are transported each week from U.S. drug markets to Mexican traffickers. Most of the money comes from drug sales in large metropolitan areas, mainly Atlanta, Chicago, Los Angeles and New York City. The money is then often smuggled across the Southwest border, typically in plastic-wrapped bundles of $20 or $100 U.S. bank notes. The money is transported by various methods, including being stashed in tires, engines and hidden compartments of cars and trucks.

U.S. law enforcement reports finding intricate hidden compartments in vehicles which contain bulk cash as well as illegally obtained firearms and drugs. While California, Florida, Michigan, Georgia and Illinois have laws banning these concealed compartments, there is no national law. I hope today's hearing will allow us to discuss potential legislative solutions.

In March 2009, Secretary of Homeland Security Janet Napolitano called on Customs and Border Protection (CBP) to inspect travelers leaving the United States for Mexico. This effort expanded CBP's primary mission of inspecting travelers who try to enter the United States. Carrying out these outbound operations is a crucial first step in curbing the flow of illicit cash and firearms from the U.S. to Mexico.

Between March 2009 and February 22, 2011, CBP seized approximately $67 million in illicit bulk cash leaving the United States at land ports of entry. 97 percent of these seizures occurred at the Southwest border. While our outbound enforcement efforts certainly are commendable, $67 million represents an incredibly small percentage of the estimated $18 to $39 billion reaching Mexican drug traffickers each year.

Of course, bulk cash smuggling is just one way of transporting money from the U.S. to Mexico. Criminals increasingly launder money from the United States to Mexico through various electronic means. While continuing to crack down on bulk cash smuggling, the United States must stay ahead of drug traffickers by going after these newer methods of money laundering.

The use of stored value cards – pre-paid gift or credit cards – is an increasingly popular means of money laundering. Remarkably, stored value is not subject to any cross-border reporting requirements. This means that an individual crossing from the United States into Mexico with thousands of dollars on pre-paid cards is not required to declare these cards at the border.

I believe that the Treasury Department has not adequately addressed stored value. The Credit CARD Act of 2009 requires the Secretary of the Treasury, in consultation with the Secretary of Homeland Security, to issue regulations regarding the sale, issuance, redemption or international transport of stored value. A Notice of Proposed Rulemaking was issued in June 2010, but did not include any proposed rules on the international transport of stored value.

I was pleased that the Treasury Department proposed a rule to make the purchase of stored value subject to Suspicious Activity Reports (SARs). This means, for example, that a Suspicious Activity Report would have to be filed if an individual purchased $2,000 on pre-paid cards at one single store and the store determined the transaction to be suspicious. Unfortunately, this rule has not yet been finalized even though the issuance of a final rule on this matter was required by February 2010. A final rule on this matter must quickly be finalized.

We simply cannot afford to lag behind drug trafficking organizations as they develop new ways to transport illegal proceeds from the United States to Mexico.

I am pleased by efforts made by Mexican President Felipe Calderón to curb bulk cash smuggling and money laundering. In 2010, President Calderón enacted into law legislation restricting the purchase of real estate with cash. Also under the new law, Mexicans are unable to purchase vehicles, boats, airplanes and luxury goods with a value greater than 100,000 pesos or $7,700 U.S. dollars. Those who violate these new regulations can be imprisoned for up to 15 years.

Finally, on both sides of the border, I believe that our efforts to understand drug trafficking organization finances are severely lacking.

In collaboration with the Calderón administration, the Obama administration should enhance authorities' and businesses' focus on understanding, mapping and tracking drug trafficking organizations' financial structures and money transfers. This should include specific tasking from law enforcement agencies and other relevant government and private sector entities to make financial information regarding drug trafficking organizations a top priority.

In the United States, we constantly ask ourselves how we can best support the Mexican government in weakening drug trafficking organizations and reducing violence in Mexico. We dedicate a great deal of time and effort going after illegal drugs and pursuing criminals. We need to equally pursue the money that drives the problem.

I look forward to hearing from the witnesses today about the most effective ways to starve Mexican drug trafficking organizations of the money that fuels them.

In: Dirty Money
Editor: Donna P. Richards ISBN: 978-1-61324-663-4

Chapter 3

OPPORTUNITIES EXIST FOR STRENGTHENING THE FEDERAL GOVERNMENT'S EFFORTS TO STEM CROSS-BORDER CURRENCY SMUGGLING

United States Government Accountability Office

Chairwoman Feinstein, Ranking Member Grassley, and Members of the Caucus:

I am pleased to be here today to discuss federal efforts to stem currency smuggling across our nation's borders. Mexican drug-trafficking organizations, terrorist organizations, and other groups with malevolent intent finance their operations by moving funds into or out of the United States. For example, a common technique used for taking proceeds from drug sales in the United States to Mexico is a method known as bulk cash smuggling.[1] The National Drug Intelligence Center (NDIC) has stated that proceeds from drug trafficking generated in this country are smuggled across the southwest border and it estimates that the proceeds total from $18 billion to $39 billion a year. NDIC also estimates that Canadian drug- trafficking organizations smuggle significant amounts of cash across the northern border from proceeds of drugs sold in the United States.

In addition to bulk cash smuggling, 21st century methods and technologies of laundering money have emerged. In 2009, NDIC stated that new financial products and technologies present unique opportunities for money launderers as well as unprecedented challenges to the intelligence, law enforcement, and regulatory communities. NDIC and others cited the use of prepaid cards or gift cards that are loaded with currency or value— also called stored value—as presenting a compact and easily transportable method to move money into and out of the United States.

U.S. Customs and Border Protection (CBP)—a major component in the Department of Homeland Security (DHS)—is the lead federal agency in charge of securing our nation's borders. In March 2009, the Secretary of Homeland Security called on CBP to help stem the flow of bulk cash and weapons moving south by inspecting travelers leaving the United States for Mexico—an effort called outbound operations. In addition, the Financial Crimes Enforcement Network (FinCEN)—a bureau in the Department of the Treasury (Treasury)—seeks to deter and detect criminal activity and safeguard the financial system from the risk that terrorists and other criminals may fund their operations through financial institutions in the United States. Among other things, FinCEN is responsible for administering laws aimed at preventing criminals from abusing U.S. financial systems.

My testimony today is based on our October 2010 report on cross-border currency smuggling and updated information on bulk cash seizures and the status of one our recommendations.[2] Like the report, it will cover the following three issues: (1) the actions CBP has taken to stem the flow of bulk cash leaving the country through land ports of entry and the challenges that remain, (2) the regulatory gaps that exist for cross-border reporting and other anti-money laundering requirements involving the use of stored value, and (3) the extent to which FinCEN has taken action to address these regulatory gaps.

To conduct our work, we visited and observed outbound operations at five ports of entry (Blaine, Washington; Buffalo, New York; El Paso, Texas; Laredo, Texas; and San Ysidro, California) that provided us examples of outbound operations on the northern and southwest border with high traffic volume. We reviewed and analyzed data on the amount of bulk cash seized from March 2009 through June 2010 and for this testimony updated bulk cash seizure data through February 22, 2011. We assessed the reliability of these data and concluded that they were sufficiently reliable for our purposes. We also reviewed CBP's policies and procedures and strategic plan for its outbound operations at land ports of entry. For this testimony, we updated the status of our recommendation to CBP that it establish a performance measure for its outbound program. We reviewed current regulations and statutes that govern issuers, sellers, and redeemers of stored value and interviewed officials or obtained information from DHS, Treasury, and the Department of Justice. We reviewed relevant legislation and proposed rules related to stored value.[3] More detailed information on our scope and methodology appears in our October 2010 report. We conducted our work in accordance with generally accepted government auditing standards.

CBP Has Established an Outbound Enforcement Program, but Further Actions Are Needed to Address Program Challenges

In March 2009, CBP reestablished the Outbound Enforcement Program within its Office of Field Operations. [4]As a result of its outbound enforcement activities, CBP seized about $67 million in illicit bulk cash leaving the country at land ports of entry—97 percent of which was seized along the southwest border— from March 2009 through February 22, 2011. Total seizures account for a small percentage of the estimated $18 billion to $39 billion in illicit proceeds being smuggled across the southwest border annually.

CBP has succeeded in establishing an Outbound Enforcement Program, but the program is in its early phases and there is a general recognition by CBP managers and officers that the agency's ability to stem the flow of bulk cash is limited because of the inherent difficulty in identifying travelers who attempt to smuggle cash. Beyond this inherent difficulty, in our October 2010 report we identified management challenges in three main areas. First, addressing limitations in staffing, infrastructure, and technology, among other things, could require substantial capital investments at all ports of entry. For example, license plate readers are available at 48 of 118 outbound lanes on the southwest border and none of the 179 outbound lanes on the northern border. Additionally, CBP officials have estimated that there are a limited number of outbound lanes networked to support computer stations or wireless computing. However, CBP lacks data on the benefits and costs of an expanded program and as a result may be unable to most effectively inform decisions on how to apply scarce resources. We recommended that CBP collect data on program costs and benefits to better inform resource decisions. CBP concurred with this recommendation and stated that it is taking action to address the recommendation.

Second, policies and procedures to ensure the safety of officers involved in outbound operations are not in place. In our October 2010 report, we recommended that CBP direct and ensure that managers at land ports of entry develop policies and procedures that address officer safety. At all five ports of entry we visited, we observed that officers used the side of the highway to conduct secondary inspections, while other vehicles moved past, potentially endangering officers. At one port of entry, officers conducted inspections of the underside of vehicles by lying on the ground with their legs exposed while traffic moved by in neighboring lanes at speeds up to approximately 25 miles per hour. CBP concurred with our recommendation and stated that it will, among other things, require each port director to develop procedures that address the safety challenges at the port of entry.

Third, CBP has developed a strategic plan for its outbound program, but it has yet to develop a performance measure that assesses the effectiveness of the program. In our October 2010 report, we recommended that CBP develop a performance measure that informs CBP management, Congress, and other stakeholders about the extent to which the Outbound Enforcement Program is effectively stemming the flow of bulk cash and other illegal goods by working with other federal law enforcement agencies. CBP concurred with our recommendation. In February 2011, CBP issued a performance measure for its outbound program that involves the amount of currency and the number of weapons seized, however, this does not fully address our recommendation because it does not measure the degree to which the program is effectively stemming the flow of bulk cash, weapons, and other goods that result from criminal activities. CBP stated in response to our recommendation that it would, among other things, investigate the use of a random sampling process in the outbound environment that would provide statistically valid compliance results for outbound operations.

REGULATORY GAPS INVOLVING CROSS- BORDER REPORTING AND OTHER ANTI-MONEY LAUNDERING REQUIREMENTS EXIST FOR STORED VALUE

Criminals can use other methods of transporting proceeds from illegal activities across the nation's borders, including stored value. Regulatory exemptions heighten the risk that criminals may use stored value to finance their operations. For example, unlike its requirements for cash, FinCEN does not require travelers to report stored value in excess of $10,000 to CBP when crossing the border. In addition, Money Services Businesses (MSBs) that offer stored value products are exempt from three key anti-money laundering provisions of the Bank Secrecy Act (BSA).[5] These exemptions involve FinCEN not specifically requiring MSBs (1) that are sole issuers, sellers, or redeemers of stored value to register with FinCEN, (2) to develop and implement a customer identification program, and (3) to report suspicious transactions involving stored value.

Together, these exemptions heighten the risk that criminals may exploit existing vulnerabilities to move criminal proceeds using stored value devices. For example, law enforcement has documented at least two mechanisms for moving currency out of the country using stored value devices. First, illegal proceeds can be loaded on stored value devices and physically carried across the border. Second, illicit proceeds can be moved out of the country by shipping stored value cards, where co-conspirators can use the cards to make purchases or to withdraw cash from local ATMs. Our report details specific examples showing how stored value can be used to transport millions of dollars in illegal proceeds across the nation's borders.

Efforts Are Underway to Address Regulatory Gaps to Stored Value, but Much Work Remains

FinCEN is in the process of developing and issuing regulations to address the risk associated with the illicit use of stored value, as required by the Credit Card Accountability Responsibility and Disclosure Act of 2009 (Credit CARD Act),[6] but much work remains and it is unclear when the agency will issue the final regulations. In June 2010, FinCEN issued a Notice of Proposed Rulemaking (NPRM) that addressed regulatory gaps in the following three areas: (1) providers of prepaid access[7] must register with FinCEN as a MSB, identify each prepaid program for which it is the provider of prepaid access, and maintain a list of its agents; (2) providers and sellers of prepaid access must establish procedures to verify the identity of a person who obtains prepaid access, including obtaining the person's name, date of birth, and address; and (3) MSBs must file reports on suspicious activities related to prepaid access. At the time of today's testimony, FinCEN had not issued the final rule.

The June 2010 NPRM, however, did not address risks related to the international transport of stored value. FinCEN stated that it plans to regulate the cross-border transport of stored value in a future rulemaking. According to

FinCEN officials, they did not address the cross-border transport of stored value in the June 2010 NPRM because addressing other regulatory gaps had a higher priority.

In our October 2010 report, we identified management challenges related to FinCEN's efforts in two areas. First, FinCEN's initial plans for issuing the final rules for stored value did not assess which risks might affect the project, prioritize risks for further analysis by assessing their probability of occurrence, or develop actions to reduce threats to the project as suggested by best practices for project management. A project management plan that is consistent with best practices could help FinCEN better manage its rulemaking effort. In addition to identifying and mitigating risks associated with the regulatory process, a project management plan could also help FinCEN (1) track and measure progress on tasks associated with completing mandated requirements and (2) identify points throughout the project to reassess efforts under way to determine whether goals and milestones are achievable or project changes are necessary. In our October 2010 report, we recommended that FinCEN update its written plan by describing, at a minimum, target dates for implementing all of the requirements under the Credit CARD Act. FinCEN concurred with our recommendation and stated that while it is challenging to identify target dates for a phased rulemaking, it will update its plans accordingly.

Second, FinCEN's approach for addressing vulnerabilities with cross-border currency smuggling and other illicit use of stored value depends, in part, on ensuring that industry complies with the new rules. In 2008, FinCEN issued guidance for examiners who monitor MSB compliance with anti-money laundering requirements. However, this guidance lacks specific information for examiners to follow when assessing MSB compliance by issuers, sellers, and redeemers of stored value. In July 2010, FinCEN officials told us that they intend to update their 2008 guidance to reflect final rules on MSBs, but they were uncertain when they will do so. In our October 2010 report, we recommended that FinCEN revise its guidance manual to include specific examination policies and procedures, including transaction testing, for examiners to follow at an MSB that issues, sells, and/or redeems stored value. FinCEN concurred with our recommendation and stated that once the initial rulemaking is finalized, it will then update the manual.

This concludes my prepared testimony. I would be pleased to respond to any questions that the members of the caucus may have.

CONTACTS AND ACKNOWLEDGMENTS

For further information regarding this testimony, please contact Richard M. Stana at (202) 512-8777 or stanar@gao.gov. Individuals who made key contributions to this testimony are Michael P. Dino, Assistant Director; Susan Quinlan, Assistant Director; David Alexander; Neil Asaba; Chuck Bausell; Willie Commons III; Kevin Copping; Ron LaDue Lake; Jan Montgomery; Jessica Orr; Jerome Sandau; Wesley Sholtes; Jonathan Smith, and Katy Trenholme.

End Notes

[1] Under 31 U.S.C. § 5332, bulk cash smuggling is defined as knowingly concealing and transporting or attempting to transport more than $10,000 in currency or monetary instruments into or out of the United States with the intent to evade the federal reporting requirements. Under 31 U.S.C. § 5316, a person or an agent or bailee of the person must file a report when the person, agent, or bailee knowingly transports, is about to transport, or has transported, monetary instruments of more than $10,000 at one time into or out of the United States.

[2] GAO, *Moving Illegal Proceeds: Challenges Exist in the Federal Government's Effort to Stem Cross-Border Currency Smuggling*, GAO-1 1-73 (Washington D.C.: Oct. 25, 2010).

[3] Amendments to the Bank Secrecy Act Regulations-Definitions and Other Regulations Relating to Prepaid Access, 75 Fed. Reg. 36589 (proposed June 28, 2010).

[4] Prior to September 11, 2001, the former U.S. Customs Service conducted outbound inspections. After this date, port directors had the discretion to continue outbound operations, but only two ports of entry continued to conduct outbound operations in a routine fashion. The Outbound Enforcement Program was reestablished, under CBP, on March 12, 2009, when the Secretary of Homeland Security called on CBP to stem the flow of cash and weapons that were being taken into Mexico through land ports of entry.

[5] Bank Secrecy Act, titles I and II of Pub. L. No. 91-508, 84 Stat. 1114 (1970) (codified as amended in 12 U.S.C. §§ 1829b, 1951-1959; 31 U.S.C. §§ 5311-5332).

[6] Pub. L. No. 111-24, 123 Stat. 1734 (2009).

[7] FinCEN proposes to revise the BSA regulations applicable to MSBs with regard to stored value by, among other things, renaming "stored value" as "prepaid access." FinCEN proposes to define "prepaid access" as an electronic device or vehicle, such as a card, plate, code, number, electronic serial number, mobile identification number, personal identification number, or other instrument that provides a portal to funds or the value of funds that have been paid in advance and can be retrievable and transferable at some point in the future.

In: Dirty Money
Editor: Donna P. Richards
ISBN: 978-1-61324-663-4

Chapter 4

Testimony of Alan Bersin, Commissioner, U.S. Customs and Border Protection, Department of Homeland Security, before the Senate Caucus on International Narcotics Control, Hearing on "Money Laundering and Bulk Cash Smuggling along the Southwest Border"

Chairman Feinstein, Co-Chairman Grassley, Members of the Caucus, it is a privilege and an honor to appear before you today to discuss the work of U.S. Customs and Border Protection (CBP), particularly the tremendous dedication of our men and women in the field, both at and between our ports of entry. In the two years since the Southwest Border Initiative was implemented, we have strengthened the security of the Southwest border in a way that many would not have thought possible. This approach to border security, along with the tireless efforts of our officers and agents in the field, has achieved historic decreases in illegal immigration; unprecedented increases in the seizure of drugs, weapons, and contraband; and strengthened and increased partnerships with Mexico on trade and travel.

My testimony today focuses on CBP's outbound operational efforts that we leverage to combat narcotics, weapons, and cash smuggling along the Southwest border.

I would like to begin by expressing my gratitude to Congress for its continued support of the mission and people of CBP. It is clear that Congress is committed to providing CBP with the resources we need to increase and maintain the security of our borders. We greatly appreciate your efforts and assistance, and I look forward to continuing to work with you on these issues in the future.

With over 58,000 employees, CBP is the largest uniformed federal law enforcement agency in the country. During fiscal years 2009 and 2010, CBP along with our counterparts at U.S. Immigration and Customs Enforcement seized more than $282 million in illegal currency, more than 7 million pounds of drugs, and more than 6,800 weapons along the Southwest border – increases of more than $73 million, more than 1 million pounds of drugs and more than 1,500 weapons compared to 2007-2008. These numbers demonstrate the effectiveness of our layered approach to security.

SOUTHWEST BORDER OPERATIONS

Southwest Border Initiatives

In March 2009, in support of the President's Southwest Border Initiative, Secretary Napolitano unveiled efforts designed to support three goals: reduce movement of contraband across the border, support Mexico's campaign to crack down on drug cartels in Mexico, and guard against the spillover of violent crime into the United States. This initiative called for additional personnel, increased intelligence capability, and better coordination with state, local and Mexican law enforcement authorities. Since the Secretary's announcement, DHS has continued working with federal, state, local and tribal authorities and the Government of Mexico to secure the Southwest border. Since the implementation of the Southwest Border Initiative, we have increased the size of the Border Patrol to more than 20,700 agents today, which is more than double the size it was in 2004. We have also begun screening southbound rail and vehicle traffic looking for the illegal weapons and cash that are helping fuel the cartel violence in Mexico. Additionally, with the aid of the $600 million supplemental appropriation that was requested by

President Obama and passed by Congress in the summer of 2010, we are continuing to add technology, manpower, and infrastructure to the border. This includes the addition of 1,000 new Border Patrol agents and 250 new CBP officers; improving our tactical communications systems; adding two new forward operating bases to improve coordination of border security activities; and adding additional CBP unmanned aircraft systems.

CBP's FY 2012 budget request continues these efforts by supporting 21,370 Border Patrol agents between the ports of entry and 21,186 CBP officers at our ports of entry who work around the clock with state, local, federal, and tribal law enforcement in targeting illicit networks trafficking in people, drugs, illegal weapons and money. Included in the request is funding to support the deployment of 300 new CBP officers and additional canine assets to port of entry operations that have recently come online. The additional CBP officers and canines will increase our enforcement capabilities to prevent the entry of unlawful people and contraband while enhancing our ability to process legitimate travelers and cargo. This reflects the largest deployment of law enforcement officers to the front line in the agency's history.

In March 2009, CBP created the Outbound Programs Division within its Office of Field Operations. This division is focused on stemming the flow of firearms, currency, stolen vehicles, and fugitives out of the United States. CBP also began scanning 100 percent of southbound rail shipments for the first time ever and increased its use of "pulse and surge" strategies for outbound operations on the Southwest border. In FY 2011, we have continued to strengthen the use of these operations along the Southwest border and to enhance our cooperative efforts with federal, state, local, and tribal law enforcement agencies. These increased Southwest border outbound security operations have yielded significant results. In fiscal years 2009 and 2010, CBP seized more than $104 million in southbound illegal currency – an increase of approximately $28 million compared to 2007-2008. In addition, in FY 2010 CBP seized more than 1,900 southbound weapons—nearly double the approximately 1,000 seized in FY 2008.

Thanks to the continued support of Congress, CBP now has 290 large-scale Non- Intrusive Inspection (NII) systems deployed to our ports of entry. Of the 290 NII systems deployed, 53 are deployed on the northern border and 142 are deployed on the Southwest border. Additionally, CBP has deployed 57 backscatter X-ray vans to Southwest border land ports of entry. To date, CBP has used the deployed systems to conduct over 32 million examinations resulting in over 7,600 narcotic seizures with a total weight of 2.4 million pounds of narcotics, and the seizure of over $19.2 million in undeclared currency. Used in combination with our layered enforcement strategy, these tools provide CBP with a significant capability to detect contraband, including illicit nuclear or radiological materials. The deployment of NII technologies has enabled our staff to efficiently process a significant volume of passengers and trade.

Increased Partnerships in Support of Southwest Border Initiatives

Working with our partners, our strategy is to secure our nation's borders by employing and enhancing our layers of defense throughout the continuum of both travelers and trade that seek to cross our borders – starting from their points of origin, through transit to the United States, arrival and entry at our borders, routes of egress, and ultimately to final destination in the United States. This strategy relies upon increased intelligence and risk-management strategies regarding the movement and flow of both travelers and trade. We accomplish our mission of expediting legal trade and travel by separating the knowns from the unknowns. This risk segmentation allows us to enhance security by focusing more attention on stopping illegitimate trade, while at the same time facilitating legitimate travel and commerce.

To further secure the Southwest border, CBP must continually increase the probability of detection and apprehension to disrupt transnational criminal organizations' ability to move drugs, weapons and illicit proceeds into and out of the United States. Doing so requires integrated planning and execution of operations across CBP, as well as seamless partnership with other government agencies and sustained collaboration with Mexico. CBP continues to assess and refine its outbound enforcement strategy to include coordinated efforts with U.S. law enforcement agencies and the Government of Mexico. These collaborative efforts assist us in enforcing U.S. export laws while depriving criminal organizations in Mexico of the illicit currency and firearms that fuel their illegal activities. In FY 2010, CBP and Mexican Customs participated in 22 joint operations along the Southwest border that resulted in the seizure of over $113,000 in currency, 23.75 kilograms of narcotics and the recovery of five stolen vehicles.

In 2003, CBP opened an Attaché office at the U.S. Embassy in Mexico City to oversee CBP operations in Mexico, including border operational support at and between the ports of entry, bilateral coordination to secure the shared border, and training for Mexican government agencies. In addition to supporting our Mexican counterparts, the Attaché's office provides subject matter expertise to the Ambassador and U.S. interagency groups within the U.S. Embassy in support of the U.S. government's trade, travel and security agendas.

Interagency cooperation at the Embassy level is essential to ensure that the right structures and mechanisms are in place to oversee the implementation of Mérida programs. DHS components have participated in the Mérida Initiative since its inception in 2007 and continue to participate in Mérida-funded programs during FY20 11. DHS has a central role in Mérida implementation in Mexico, and prioritizes support on dismantling transnational criminal organizations, securing the Southwest border, training and assisting vetted units, and bulk cash smuggling. DHS participation in the Mérida Initiative supports the provision of equipment, training, and other capacity building efforts in Mexico.

As we have enhanced our collaboration with our neighbors to the south, CBP also has continued to build upon our partnerships within the United States. In September 2009, we initiated the Operation Alliance to Combat Transnational Threats (ACTT)—a collaborative enforcement effort to leverage the capabilities and resources of more than 60 federal, state, local and tribal agencies in Arizona and from the Government of Mexico to combat individuals and criminal organizations that pose a threat to communities on both sides of the border. While ACTT's initial focus is on Arizona, as it continues to evolve, focused operations will transition to other operational corridors.

CBP continues to work with its partners in the Drug Enforcement Administration (DEA) and the Southwest Border High Intensity Drug Trafficking Area program to expand the national License Plate Reader (LPR) initiative to exploit intelligence on drug traffickers and drug trafficking organizations. The LPR initiative utilizes established locations to gather information regarding travel patterns and border nexus on drug traffickers for intelligence-driven operations and interdictions. We have also established positions at the El Paso Intelligence Center (EPIC), the Organized Crime Drug Enforcement Task Force Fusion Center, and the DEA Special Operations Division and continue to participate in other multi-agency task forces such the ICE Border Enforcement Security Teams and Border Intelligence Centers targeting drugs, weapons and currency across the Southwest border.

These partnerships enhance interaction with the Intelligence Community and law enforcement agencies to more effectively facilitate the collection, analysis, and dissemination of actionable intelligence in support of drug trafficking and money laundering investigations all along the Southwest border.

Intelligence and Operational Coordination

CBP, in cooperation with the DHS Office of Intelligence and Analysis, continues its work to become a more integrated, intelligence-driven organization. Intelligence gathering and predictive analysis require new collection and processing capabilities. CBP's Office of Intelligence and Operations Coordination (OIOC) is designing systems to process and analyze imagery collected from aircraft and other platforms. Though not specific to Southwest border security efforts, CBP is also developing the Analytical Framework for Intelligence, a set of data processing tools that improves the ability of CBP and other DHS analysts to effectively detect, locate, and analyze terrorist networks, drug trafficking networks, and other transnational threats.

These intelligence and operational coordination initiatives complement our existing technology programs.

In March 2010, CBP opened the first Intelligence and Operations Coordination Center (IOCC) in Tucson, Arizona. The IOCC serves as the development platform for CBP to operate joint intelligence operations that include coordination with our other federal, state and local law enforcement partners. CBP is building more focused discipline into our intelligence operations by incorporating post-seizure analysis techniques and interagency coordination efforts to link intelligence and law enforcement information for our operations and interdictions into our training and standard operating procedures. These efforts are helping CBP develop into a more fully integrated, intelligence-driven organization.

CONCLUSION

Chairman Feinstein, Co-Chairman Grassley, and members of the Caucus: thank you again for this opportunity to testify about the work of U.S. Customs and Border Protection, and particularly about our efforts to increase security along the Southwest border. CBP is committed to aggressively and proactively securing our nation's borders and safeguarding our way of life. Your continued support of CBP has led to significant improvements in the security of our borders, and made our nation safer. I will be glad to answer any questions you may have.

In: Dirty Money
Editor: Donna P. Richards
ISBN: 978-1-61324-663-4

Chapter 5

STATEMENT OF KUMAR C. KIBBLE, DEPUTY DIRECTOR, U.S. IMMIGRATION AND CUSTOMS ENFORCEMENT, DEPARTMENT OF HOMELAND SECURITY, BEFORE THE SENATE CAUCUS ON INTERNATIONAL NARCOTICS CONTROL, HEARING ON "MONEY LAUNDERING AND BULK CASH SMUGGLING ALONG THE SOUTHWEST BORDER"

INTRODUCTION

Chairman Feinstein, Co-Chairman Grassley, and distinguished Members of the Caucus: on behalf of Secretary Napolitano and Assistant Secretary Morton, I would like to thank you for the opportunity to discuss the efforts of U S Immigration and Customs Enforcement (ICE) to combat cross-border smuggling organizations and the illicit proceeds used to fund their criminal activities. ICE has the most expansive investigative authority and largest force of investigators in the Department of Homeland Security (DHS). We protect national security and uphold public safety by targeting transnational criminal networks and terrorist organizations that seek to exploit our borders and America's legitimate trade, travel, and financial systems. Recognizing that partnerships are essential, ICE works closely across agency and international boundaries with our law enforcement partners at the foreign, federal, tribal, state and local level creating a united front to disrupt and dismantle transnational criminal organizations.

ICE's expertise in combating criminal organizations that exploit vulnerabilities in the sea, air, and land environments has proven essential in countering the smuggling of narcotics, money, dangerous goods, people and materials that threaten the well-being of the United States. Our law enforcement presence is global and ICE has a wide network of agents in attaché offices at embassies and consulates worldwide, all working in concert to target transnational criminal organizations. I am proud of these agents who work closely with their foreign counterparts to dismantle criminal organizations before they reach our nation's borders.

I would be remiss if I did not mention the recent brutal attack on two of our Special Agents who were shot in the line of duty while on mission in central Mexico in late February. ICE Special Agent Jaime J. Zapata lost his life and Special Agent Victor Avila was seriously injured in the service of our country. Sadly, this tragedy is a stark reminder of the dangers confronted and the sacrifices made every day by our nation's law enforcement officers, and our hearts and prayers continue to go out to the victims and their families. Special Agent Zapata died fighting for what was right and will forever be remembered as a man of courage and honor. ICE is committed to continuing to assist the ongoing Mexican investigation to ensure that the perpetrators of this crime are brought to justice.

I want to stress that our working relationship with fellow law enforcement and civilian agencies in Mexico remains extremely positive and well-coordinated. As an example of the increasing coordination and cooperation, I would like to highlight the Bi-National Criminal Proceeds Study, which was released in June 2010.

This study, organized by ICE and commissioned by the Department of Homeland Security's Office of Counternarcotics Enforcement, was prepared in collaboration with the Government of Mexico and other federal agencies and underscores our shared commitment to fighting transnational criminal organizations. This bi-national study reveals the means by which transnational criminal enterprises move criminal proceeds from the United States into Mexico and beyond. The information outlined in the study—including critical assessments of money collection sites, transport routes, and chokepoints—enables the United States and Mexico to strategically target our law enforcement operations. The study and its findings are being addressed and implemented as part of several bi-national planning and strategic working groups. ICE participates in and/or leads these groups, which provide a forum for U.S. and Mexican law enforcement to coordinate, de-conflict and enhance significant criminal investigations of mutual interest.

Southwest Border Initiatives

In March 2009, the Administration launched the Southwest Border Initiative to bring unprecedented focus and intensity to Southwest border security, coupled with a reinvigorated, smart and effective approach to enforcing immigration laws in the interior of our country. In support of this initiative, ICE, through the Border Enforcement Security Task Forces (BEST) has targeted considerable resources at the Southwest border to interdict contraband, firearms, ammunition, undeclared currency, stolen vehicles, human smuggling, transnational criminal organizations, tunnel detection and other border crime at and between ports of entry along the Southwest border.

In FY 2010, ICE deployed special agents to high-risk locations, including Tijuana and Monterrey, and initiated 15,013 investigations along the Southwest Border — an increase of 16 percent over FY 2009.

Additionally, with the aid of the $600 million supplemental appropriation that was requested by President Obama and passed by Congress in the summer of 2010, ICE is placing over 250 positions, including special agents, investigators and intelligence analysts, along the border. Indeed, ICE now has one quarter of its personnel assigned to the Southwest border, more agents and officers along the border than ever before.

Targeting Transnational Criminal Organizations and Pursuing Money Laundering and Bulk Cash Smugging Investigations

One of the most effective methods for dismantling transnational criminal organizations is to attack the criminal proceeds that fund their operations. ICE targets members and associates of transnational criminal organizations that seek to exploit vulnerabilities in the trade, travel and financial systems to earn, move and store their illicit proceeds. ICE investigations utilize a "supply chain attack" strategy designed to create cascading failures within a criminal organization by simultaneously targeting multiple components within the organization.

The combination of successful financial investigations, reporting requirements under the Bank Secrecy Act, and anti-money laundering compliance efforts by financial institutions has strengthened formal financial systems and forced criminal organizations to seek other means to transport illicit funds across our borders. ICE, as the investigative agency with jurisdiction over all border crimes, investigates bulk cash smuggling violations, which are predicated on the failure to file a Currency and Monetary Instrument Report (CMIR) with U.S. Customs and Border Protection (CBP).

ICE's National Bulk Cash Smuggling Center

On August 11, 2009, ICE officially launched the National Bulk Cash Smuggling Center (BCSC), which is a 24/7 investigative support and operations facility co-located at the Law Enforcement Support Center in Williston, Vermont. Since its launch, the BCSC has undertaken a full assessment of the bulk cash smuggling threat and has developed a strategic plan to address the problem.

The BCSC utilizes a systems approach to identify vulnerabilities and disrupt the flow of illicit bulk cash at the Southwest border and beyond. By analyzing the movement of bulk cash as a systematic process, ICE develops enforcement operations to defeat the various smuggling methodologies currently employed by trafficking organizations. This approach allows us to more efficiently and effectively utilize our interdiction and investigative resources.

To date, the BCSC has initiated 329 investigations, which have resulted in more than 35 arrests and more than 70 seizures. In July and August 2010, ICE Special Agents working in conjunction with state and local law enforcement officers seized more than 4,000 pounds of narcotics stemming from a BCSC investigation into a criminal organization based in New York City and Philadelphia that was responsible for the movement of bulk cash across the Southwest border to Mexico. To date, this investigation has resulted in four arrests and the seizure of more than $3 million in narcotics proceeds. ICE continues to work with its partners in Arizona, Maryland, Texas and New York to identify additional associates of this trafficking organization.

ICE is further cooperating with both foreign and domestic law enforcement partners to disrupt the criminal organizations that are smuggling narcotics into the United States and smuggling bulk cash shipments out. The expanding relationship between ICE's BCSC and the Drug Enforcement Administration's (DEA) El Paso Intelligence Center (EPIC) is a key component of these efforts.

The relationship between the BCSC and EPIC is mutually supportive. The respective missions have distinct but complementary roles in combating the flow of illicit finance that is fueling violence in Mexico. The BCSC and EPIC are currently coordinating the establishment of the Bulk Cash Smuggling Center Intake & Analysis Section (BCSC I&A) at EPIC, which will be led by ICE with participation from our law enforcement partners. The BCSC I&A will function as a single point of contact for state and local law enforcement entities to report bulk currency interdictions and receive immediate real-time analysis and support. In addition, the BCSC has invited EPIC to staff a position(s) at the BCSC to further strengthen the relationship between the two centers.

Operation Pacific Rim

Operation Pacific Rim is an ICE-led investigation, with the assistance of DEA and FBI, which dismantled one of the most powerful and sophisticated bulk cash and drug smuggling super-cartels in the world. This super cartel was responsible for nearly half of the cocaine smuggled from Colombia into the United States between 2003 and 2009: approximately 912 tons with an estimated street value of $24 billion.

Operation Pacific Rim originally targeted suspicious containerized shipments of fertilizer at Colombian seaports in Buenaventura and Cartagena. In September 2009, ICE special agents, working closely with the Colombian National Police and the Mexican Secretariat of Public Security, intercepted $41 million in bundles of shrink-wrapped bulk cash concealed within shipments of fertilizer intercepted at seaports in Colombia and Mexico.

Subsequent to the $41 million seizure, special agents from ICE Attaché offices in Bogota and Mexico City expanded the scope of the investigation by identifying the bulk cash and drug smuggling routes utilized by the cartel. ICE Special Agents eventually obtained enough information to launch an offensive across three continents, resulting in the capture of the leadership and other high ranking members of the Pacific Rim Cartel. During the arrest of these individuals, ICE developed and utilized cooperating defendants that led to the seizure of an additional $163.8 million in illicit bulk currency, 3.3 tons of cocaine, $179 million in assets, and $37 million in criminal forfeiture warrants. ICE's efforts helped lead to 22 indictments, 21 arrests, and nine convictions.

Operation Firewall

ICE's Operation Firewall disrupts the movement and smuggling of bulk cash en route to the border, at the border, and internationally via commercial and private passenger vehicles, commercial airline shipments, airline passengers and pedestrians. Since 2005, we have enhanced Operation Firewall efforts to include surge operations targeting the movement of bulk cash destined for the Southwest border to be smuggled into Mexico. In fiscal year 2010, Operation Firewall efforts in Mexico resulted in seizures totaling over $6.1 million, the arrest of 13 couriers and the initiation of over a dozen joint criminal investigations. Since its inception in 2005, Operation Firewall has resulted in more than 5,100 seizures totaling more than $494 million and the arrest of more than 1,000 individuals. These efforts include more 300 international seizures totaling more than $236 million and over 215 international arrests.

In addition to our international investigations, domestic Operation Firewall efforts assist us in documenting and gathering intelligence on how organizations involved in bulk cash smuggling operate. For example, in May 2010, during a routine traffic stop, the ICE Special Agent in Charge office in St. Louis and the Illinois State Police found and subsequently seized $91,550 that was concealed within several natural voids in a vehicle. The subjects admitted that the currency was proceeds from the sale of cocaine, and that they were being paid to drive the currency back to Mexico. These individuals also admitted to having been involved in the smuggling of narcotics and currency about once every two weeks for several years. One of the occupants added that the Mexico-based criminal organization with which he was affiliated regularly exploited his criminal record by using him as a "decoy vehicle" as he entered the United States from Mexico. He stated that while CBP officers questioned and searched his vehicle, other vehicles laden with cocaine were able to pass undetected. Both individuals pled guilty to narcotics-related offenses. One of the individuals was sentenced to 140 months in prison, while the other individual awaits sentencing.

Operation Cornerstone

In July 2003, ICE launched its Cornerstone Outreach Initiative to work in partnership with the private sector to systematically and strategically identify and close down vulnerabilities in financial systems through which criminals launder their illicit proceeds. ICE builds both domestic and international partnerships by sharing law enforcement trends and methods with businesses and industries that manage the systems terrorists and criminal organizations seek to exploit. .

ICE provides training to the private sector on how to identify and prevent exploitation by criminal organizations. ICE special agents serve as subject matter experts in various types of money laundering methods, including fraudulent schemes, money service businesses, casinos, non-cash negotiable instruments, alternate remitters, charities, outbound currency initiatives, organized retail crime and schemes to pay illegal alien workers.

Through January 31, 2011, ICE special agents conducted approximately 9,818 Cornerstone outreach and training presentations to approximately 193,350 participants worldwide. Through fiscal year 2010, ICE's outreach efforts have resulted in the initiation of 416 criminal investigations that led to 270 arrests, 234 indictments, 183 convictions, and the seizure of nearly $157 million.

Prepaid and Stored Value Cards and Other Emerging Methods

The terms "prepaid card" and "stored value card" (collectively "PP/SVCs") are commonly used in reference to any card that represents money stored on or accessible by a card to facilitate a consumer's purchases of goods, services, or further conversion to cash through an ATM. These cards may be "open loop" or "closed loop." Open loop cards are usually network- branded, often reloadable, and can be used at point of sale terminals and ATMs anonymously. Closed loop cards, on the other hand, are designated for use at a specific merchant, typically have load limits, and cannot be converted back to cash. Examples of closed loop PP/SVCs include gift cards, mass transit cards, and prepaid phone cards.

According to the 2007 U.S. National Money Laundering Strategy, "stored value cards (sometimes referred to as prepaid cards) are an emerging cash alternative for both legitimate consumers and money launderers alike." Of the two types, money launderers appear to prefer the open loop PP/SVCs because of their capability to be used at point of sale terminals, their wide acceptance by hotels and car rental agencies, and their portability. These cards enable the user to obtain cash from ATMs worldwide without going through a currency exchange. Additionally, cards issued by offshore financial institutions—and therefore not subject to U.S. reporting requirements—are widely available on the internet, including cards with very high load limits. PP/SVCs may be attractive to money launderers and smugglers as an alternative to bulk cash not only because of their small size and portability, but also because they are not expressly defined as monetary instruments under U.S. statutes and regulations and, therefore, they are not expressly and specifically subject to the CMIR reporting requirements or the potential bulk cash smuggling and structuring violations that stem from this requirement.

An October 2010 Financial Action Task Force (FATF) report titled "New Payment Methods" states"... it appears that since 2006, a limited number of cases involving cross-border transport of prepaid cards has started to emerge. The lack of examples can be explained by the fact that prepaid cards are not considered monetary instruments in most jurisdictions and that it is very difficult for customs officers to easily differentiate prepaid cards from regular credit cards given that both share very similar physical attributes." ICE contributed to the FATF report, and in order to provide much needed information to law enforcement, ICE deve loped and distributed a pamphlet to inform and educate ICE personnel, as well as federal, state, local and foreign law enforcement partners. The pamphlet, titled "Emerging Trends in Money Laundering: Pre Paid Cards," provides an overview ofhow PP/SVCs function and outlines specific vulnerabilities associated with them. ICE also delivers instruction on the money laundering vulnerabilities associated with the misuse ofPP/SVCs at domestic and international money laundering conferences and seminars sponsored by organizations like the Asia Pacific Economic Cooperation group, the FATF, the World Customs Organization, the Organization of American States and the United Nations Office ofDrugs and Crime, among others.

As a result of ICE's outreach efforts, domestic law enforcement agencies are now voluntarily reaching out to ICE when they encounter these cards. Over the last six months, authorities in New Mexico have encountered two separate instances where hundreds ofPP/SVCs were found concealed in a compartment similar to those used to conceal cash, drugs and other contraband. The cards are also being used by criminal organizations to cover "expenses" incurred by their couriers as they transport cash, drugs and other contraband across the country. Customs authorities in Jamaica recently contacted the ICE Attache Kingston requesting assistance with hundreds of U.S. issued PP/SVCs they are finding in mail coming from the United States. These cards are associated with advance-fee schemes, which primarily target elderly U.S. citizens.

The Credit CARD Act of 2009 mandated that the U.S. Department of the Treasury (Treasury), in consultation with DHS, address the risks associated with these cards. Section 503 of the Act required that Treasury issue regulations in final form within 270 days implementing the Bank Secrecy Act regarding the "sale, issuance, redemption, or international transport of stored value," and that such regulations regarding international transport of stored value may include subjecting these cards to the cross-border reporting requirement. ICE has met with Treasury's Financial Crimes Enforcement Network on multiple occasions since the Act was enacted on May 22, 2009, to ensure that the regulations, which have not yet been issued, adequately mitigate the risks associated with the international transport of PP/SVCs.

ICE'S EFFORTS TO COMBAT KLEPTOCRACY

Through our Foreign Corruption Investigations Group in Miami, ICE works with foreign governments to conduct investigations into the laundering of proceeds emanating from foreign public corruption, bribery or embezzlement, also referred to as "kleptocracy." The objective is to prevent these funds from entering the U.S. financial infrastructure, to seize identified assets in the United States, and to repatriate these funds to the proper foreign government authorities. ICE participates in the Anti-Kleptocracy Working Group, chaired by the National Security Council and focused on the U.S. government's response to large-scale corruption by public officials. ICE has played an integral role in the development of the working group strategy as ICE is uniquely positioned as the U.S. cross-border investigative agency possessing international money laundering expertise, immigration authorities, experience in complex financial investigations, and extensive international investigative assets.

One example of ICE's multinational working relationship is the assistance provided to Taiwanese authorities in their efforts to recover bribery proceeds paid to former President Chen Shui-bian and his family. On July 14, 2010, as a result of joint efforts between ICE, the Department of Justice and the Taiwan Supreme Prosecutors Office, the U.S. government filed civil forfeiture complaints against properties in New York and Virginia that represent a portion of the approximately $6 million in illegal bribes paid to the former president and his wife by a financial services company. The funds used to purchase the properties were moved from Taiwan to the United States by using shell companies obtained at off-shore banking centers in the Caribbean and Switzerland. Former President Shui-bian and his wife were convicted of bribery, embezzlement and money laundering by the Supreme Court of Taiwan and sentenced to 20 years in prison. Additional indictments are pending in Taiwan.

CONCLUSION

Chairman Feinstein, Co-Chairman Grassley, and distinguished Members of the Caucus, thank you again for the opportunity to testify today and for your continued support of ICE and its law enforcement mission. ICE is committed to stemming cross-border criminal organizations and the illegal proceeds used to fund their criminal activities through the various efforts I have discussed today. I appreciate your interest in these important issues and look forward to continuing to work with you. I would be pleased to answer to answer any questions you may have.

In: Dirty Money
Editor: Donna P. Richards

ISBN: 978-1-61324-663-4

Chapter 6

STATEMENT OF ASSOCIATE DIRECTOR FOR REGULATORY POLICY AND PROGRAMS, JAMAL EL-HINDI, FINANCIAL CRIMES ENFORCEMENT NETWORK, BEFORE THE SENATE CAUCUS ON INTERNATIONAL NARCOTICS CONTROL, HEARING ON "MONEY LAUNDERING AND BULK CASH SMUGGLING ALONG THE SOUTHWEST BORDER"

Chairman Feinstein, Co-Chairman Grassley, and distinguished Members of the Caucus, thank you for the opportunity to appear before you today to discuss the Financial Crimes Enforcement Network's (FinCEN) ongoing role under the leadership of the Under Secretary of the Treasury for Terrorism and Financial Intelligence, in the Administration's efforts to stem the flow of illicit proceeds along the southwest border. We appreciate the Caucus' interest in this important issue, and your continued support of our efforts to help prevent illegal financial activity in this region.

I am also pleased to be testifying with my colleagues from the Department of Homeland Security (DHS) and the Government Accountability Office (GAO). Each of them plays an important role in the global fight against money laundering and terrorist financing, and our collaboration on these issues along the southwest border has greatly improved the effectiveness of our efforts.

Each of the major initiatives that I will touch upon in my testimony are among FinCEN's contributions to the Administration's National Southwest Border Counternarcotics Strategy[i], and the 2010 Implementation Update of that Strategy.[ii]

FinCEN's mission is to enhance U.S. national security, detect criminal activity, and safeguard financial systems from abuse by promoting transparency in the U.S. and international financial systems. FinCEN works to achieve its mission through a broad range of interrelated strategies, including:

- Administering the Bank Secrecy Act (BSA) - the United States' primary anti-money laundering (AML)/counter-terrorist financing (CFT) regulatory regime;
- Supporting law enforcement, intelligence, and regulatory agencies through the sharing and analysis of financial intelligence; and,
- Building global cooperation and technical expertise among financial intelligence units throughout the world.

To accomplish these activities, FinCEN employs a team comprised of approximately 320 dedicated federal employees, including analysts, regulatory specialists, international specialists, technology experts, lawyers, administrators, managers, and federal agents.

FinCEN's main goal in administering the BSA is to increase the transparency of the U.S. financial system so that money laundering, terrorist financing, and other economic crime can be detected, investigated, prosecuted, and ultimately prevented. Our ability to work closely with our regulatory, law enforcement, international, and industry partners promotes consistency across our regulatory regime and better protects the U.S. financial system.

Mitigating Money Laundering Vulnerabilities in Prepaid Access Devices

One of our biggest challenges as a regulator of financial institutions is striking the right balance between the costs and benefits of regulation. Recognizing the emergence of sophisticated payment methods and the potential for abuse by criminal actors, several years ago FinCEN began working with our law enforcement and regulatory counterparts and the industries we regulate to study the stored value/prepaid card industry in the context of expanding AML obligations to emerging payment systems. While regulations covering money services businesses in this sector have been in place since 1999, those requirements were not as comprehensive as the requirements for other sectors; this less comprehensive approach was appropriate at the time as the prepaid/stored value industry was new and there was a desire not to squelch its development. Over time, however, it was clear that more comprehensive regulations were needed.

Recognizing the importance and value of bringing a cross-section of experts together to study this issue, in May 2008 FinCEN formally established a subcommittee to focus on stored value issues within the Bank Secrecy Act Advisory Group (BSAAG). The BSAAG is a Congressionally-chartered forum[iii] that brings together representatives from the financial industry, law enforcement, and the regulatory community to advise FinCEN in its regulatory functions. The stored value subcommittee provides a comprehensive panel of experts available to consult on these issues and from whom a body of empirical information is regularly gathered and exchanged.

Prepaid access is attractive to customers who do not have similar easy-to-obtain options for non- cash payments or the ability to conduct transactions remotely. But the ease with which prepaid access can be obtained and used, combined with the potential for the relatively high velocity of money moving through accounts involving prepaid access, the potential in some cases for anonymity, and the lack of a full regulatory framework, may make it particularly attractive to illicit actors. Criminals value the ability to receive and distribute a significant amount of funds without being subject to many of the reporting or recordkeeping requirements that would apply to similar transactions using cash or involving an ordinary demand deposit account at a bank. These are among the reasons FinCEN believes that the risks and appropriate regulatory framework to attempt to mitigate them is to consider prepaid access as a type of money transmission.

The framework for money transmission – and that which we propose for prepaid access – is an activity-based test. More specifically, we are looking at the ability to introduce value and to realize that value at a subsequent time, at a different place, or by a different person, for a subset of the original amount, or some combination thereof.

In furtherance of the above, FinCEN began to take formal steps to address this industry sector -- including seeking public comment on how stored value should be defined and related issues in the proposed rule, Amendment to the Bank Secrecy Act Regulations – Definitions and Other Regulations Relating to Money Services Businesses.[iv] After we had begun efforts to revise our regulations, on May 22, 2009, President Obama signed the Credit Card Accountability, Responsibility, and Disclosure (CARD) Act of 2009.[v] Section 503 of the CARD Act directs FinCEN, as administrator of the BSA, to issue regulations regarding the sale, issuance, redemption, or international transport of stored value, including prepaid devices such as plastic cards, mobile phones, electronic serial numbers, key fobs and/or other mechanisms that provide access to funds that have been paid for in advance and are retrievable and transferable. Although FinCEN had taken steps toward more comprehensive regulations for the prepaid/stored value sector before the CARD Act became law, the statute accelerated our timeframe.

After extensive study, FinCEN issued its notice of proposed rulemaking (NPRM) which proposed new rules that would establish a comprehensive BSA/AML regulatory framework for non-bank stored value providers, which our proposal now refers to as "prepaid access." In developing this NPRM, we consulted with the Department of Homeland Security and various other law enforcement and regulatory agencies throughout the process, meeting throughout 2009-2010 with larger and smaller groups of stakeholders as often as three to four times each month to collaborate on these issues and to solicit input for moving forward.

Under FinCEN's proposal, non-bank providers of prepaid access would be subject to comprehensive BSA regulations similar to depository institutions. To make BSA reports and records valuable and meaningful, the proposed changes would impose obligations on a party responsible for predominant oversight and control, as well as others who might be in a position to provide meaningful information to regulators and law enforcement. Depository institutions would retain AML obligations for most bank-issued prepaid cards.

Among the major features in the proposal are:

- Renaming "stored value" as "prepaid access" to allow for future changes in technology and prepaid devices;
- Making this newly defined "provider" of prepaid access a responsible party subject to regulation;
- Placing program requirements on providers of prepaid access, including registration, suspicious activity reporting, customer information recordkeeping, and new transactional recordkeepi ng requirements;
- Establishing requirements for sellers of prepaid access; and,

- Exempting certain categories of prepaid access products and services posing lower risks of money laundering and terrorist financing from certain requirements.

This last aspect assists our efforts to achieve the right balance. FinCEN believes that certain prepaid programs operate in such a way as to reduce potential money laundering threats and are therefore generally not subject to the provisions of the NPRM. Such products include payroll cards, government benefits cards, health care access cards, closed loop cards, and low dollar products with strong safeguards in place.

Other risk variables - such as whether a product is reloadable, can be transferred to other consumers, or can be used to transfer funds outside the country - were all things that we identified through our extensive regulatory, law enforcement, and industry consultations. With the NPRM, we asked the general public to help validate whether we have found the right balance so that higher-risk persons and products will be appropriately regulated while lower-risk products would not be subject to undue regulatory obligations or constraints.

The proposed regulation is designed to be flexible and to accommodate new technologies as they emerge. Prepaid access can include cards, electronic serial numbers or codes, mobile phones, key fobs and other yet-to-be-invented devices. Now that the comment period has ended and the information received has been thoroughly reviewed, we are diligently working to finalize the rule as quickly as possible, while continuing our obligation to strike the correct balance between law enforcement needs and a meaningful, workable regulation. With respect to timing, we recognize that the 270-day statutory deadline for finalizing the regulation has expired, and completing it remains a top FinCEN priority.

Strategic Collaboration with the Government of Mexico

FinCEN has a strong history of cooperation with its counterpart financial intelligence unit (FIU) in Mexico -- the Unidad de Inteligencia Financiera (UIF) -- dating back to 1994 when FinCEN completed negotiations of an agreement to exchange information on financial crimes that was signed by then-Secretary of the Treasury Lloyd Bentsen together with then-Mexican

Finance Minister Pedro Aspe Armella. For 15 years, FinCEN's ongoing work with the UIF demonstrates the mutual commitment and deep level of cooperation between our two countries. The bilateral cooperation to exchange information relating to cross-border threats and thereby further law enforcement cooperation is leveraged through the participation of FinCEN and the UIF in the Egmont Group[vi] of FIUs from over 100 jurisdictions around the world. Representatives from FinCEN and the UIF have long been active in building this international network, and both countries have served as chairmen of the Egmont Group in the past. Membership in the Egmont Group provides a structured process for making requests for tactical, case-related financial information from one nation to another outside of other international legal agreements such as mutual legal assistance treaties (MLATs) and Letters Rogatory. In recent years, both agencies expanded cooperation and information sharing to new levels, agreeing to work jointly to support bi-national law enforcement efforts to combat the illicit finance activity of the Mexican cartels and their cohorts in the United States. FinCEN also has deepened its cooperation with its Mexican counterpart responsible for AML/CFT regulations, the National Banking and Securities Commission (CNBV).

For example, FinCEN and the UIF completed a joint study in 2010 of cross-border currency flows and U.S. banknote activity in Mexico. The effort developed a model for constructive sharing of financial information based on a relationship of shared goals and mutual benefits. The findings of the study helped inform the Mexican government's June 2010 decision to implement regulations restricting U.S. dollar acceptance by Mexican financial institutions. The FinCEN/UIF study also identified money laundering targets that were referred to U.S. and Mexican law enforcement agencies for investigative follow-up. The success of this study led to the detail of a senior FinCEN analyst to Mexico to work directly with the UIF in 2010.

FinCEN Analyst Deployed to Mexico

FinCEN's multi-year assignment of a senior analyst to Mexico has helped to facilitate closer cooperation and collaboration between FinCEN and the UIF, with the expected result of improving the quality and quantity of joint projects and facilitating the sharing of sensitive information and money laundering targets with U.S. law enforcement agencies, particularly U.S.

Immigration and Customs Enforcement (ICE), the Drug Enforcement Administration (DEA), Federal Bureau of Investigation (FBI) and Criminal Investigation division of the Internal Revenue Service (IRS-CI). The FinCEN analyst embedded in the UIF has proven to be a force- multiplier by utilizing his unique position to support many cases of joint interest to the U.S. and Mexican authorities. For example, the FinCEN analyst is providing analytical support to 12 bilateral law enforcement investigations, all of which are related to narcotics and contraband money laundering cases. The FinCEN analyst in Mexico continues to work closely with colleagues at FinCEN headquarters and also complements the work of our longstanding analyst based in Texas at the Southwest border High Intensity Financial Crime Area (HIFCA). Furthermore, in April 2010, FinCEN launched an effort with the support of the Office of National Drug Control Policy (ONDCP) to more consistently engage with and support financial aspects of investigations in the High Intensity Drug Trafficking Areas (HIDTAs). A focus of the coming year will be training analysts and ensuring ongoing points of contact in the interagency coordinating groups in the HIDTAs.

Mexican Regulations Imposing Restrictions on Mexican Banks for Transactions in U.S. Currency

As previously mentioned, on June 15, 2010, the Mexican finance ministry announced new AML regulations to restrict the amounts of physical cash (banknotes and coins) denominated in U.S. dollars that Mexican banks may receive.[vii] Shortly following this announcement, FinCEN issued a public Advisory[viii] to financial institutions advising them of these important actions taken by Mexican authorities. The Advisory outlines several potential direct and indirect effects – some of which we are already observing, and others that we continue to monitor for and assess. For example, in analyzing cross-border currency flows between the United States and Mexico, we have observed notable changes, but other potential impacts, such as increased pressure to place criminal proceeds in the U.S. financial system, or diversion of currency to other countries in the region, are more difficult to directly quantify. The Advisory also requests that filers include a special keyword in Suspicious Activity Report (SAR) narratives ("MX RESTRICTION") where the filer believes suspicious financial activity could be related to the regulatory change in Mexico. This has allowed FinCEN to more easily monitor for potential shifts in suspicious activity or emerging money laundering trends.

As Mexican banks must now limit the amount of U.S. dollars they receive from their customers, they are sending less cash back to the United States through bank channels, such as wholesale banknote shipments. Consistent with reporting from Mexican authorities and industry groups, wholesale banknote repatriation from Mexico to the United States has declined significantly following the implementation of the U.S. dollar cash restrictions. As reported on Currency Transaction Reports (CTRs) that are filed by depository institutions, currency repatriation from Mexican banks and licensed casas de cambio declined 64 percent in the fourth quarter of 2010 (the first full quarter after the Mexican regulations took effect) compared to the same period in 2009 (representing an annual decline of 37 percent comparing year-end 2010 to 2009).

Moving forward, we must also be mindful that as Mexican financial institutions limit their acceptance of U.S. dollar transactions, money flows -- particularly those related to narcotics trafficking or organized crime -- could instead be diverted from Mexico to other countries in the region. Moreover, trends in other forms of criminal activity such as trade-based money laundering could potentially rise. Vigilance is paramount and we will continue monitoring BSA data and other sources for changes in broader money laundering trends that may result, and we will continue to foster collaboration with our counterpart FIUs on this issue, including partners from Colombia and Guatemala who have hosted a number of multilateral FIU meetings on this topic.

Proposed Regulatory Requirement for Financial Institutions to Report Cross-Border Electronic Transmittals of Funds

In September 2010, FinCEN submitted an NPRM that would require certain depository institutions and money services businesses (MSBs) to report records to FinCEN of certain cross- border electronic transmittals of funds (CBETF). Current regulations already require that these financial institutions maintain and make available, but not affirmatively report, essentially the same CBETF information. FinCEN issued this proposal to meet the requirements of the Intelligence Reform and Terrorism Prevention Act of 2004 (IRTPA).

Section 6302 of IRTPA[ix] directed the Secretary of the Treasury to study the feasibility of "requiring such financial institutions as the Secretary determines to be appropriate to report to the Financial Crimes Enforcement Network certain cross-border electronic transmittals of funds, if the Secretary determines that reporting of such transmittals is reasonably necessary to conduct the efforts of the Secretary against money laundering and terrorist financing."

Prior to publishing the NPRM, FinCEN conducted an extensive study of the technical feasibility to the government of imposing such a requirement and in January of 2007 published the congressionally-mandated report *Feasibility of a Cross-Border Electronic Funds Transfer Reporting System under the Bank Secrecy Act*[x] that affirmed the feasibility of the reporting system. FinCEN, with the participation of both the financial services industry and law enforcement, then conducted a follow on study on *Implications and Benefits of Cross-Border Funds Transmittal Reporting*[xi] to determine and quantify both the benefits to the public of the system and the costs to parties affected by any such potential regulatory requirement.

The proposal will produce valuable data for law enforcement agencies by having first-in and last- out depository institutions (those institutions that are the first to receive funds transferred electronically from outside the United States or the last U.S. institution to transmit funds internationally) to report all such transmittals of funds. MSBs that conduct CBETF will be required to report international transactions equal to or in excess of $1,000. FinCEN estimates that fewer than 300 depository institutions and 700 MSBs will be subject to this requirement.

FinCEN is also proposing to require an annual filing by all depository institutions of a list of taxpayer identification numbers of accountholders who transmitted or received a CBETF. This additional information will facilitate the utilization of the CBETF data, in particular as part of efforts to combat tax evasion by those who would seek to hide assets in offshore accounts. The comment period for the NPRM ended on December 29, 2010 and we are currently reviewing the comments received.

Bi-National Partnering to Combat Bulk Cash Smuggling

I would also like to share with you that in April 2010, FinCEN supported DHS and the Government of Mexico to complete a U.S.-Mexico Bi-national Criminal Proceeds Study. The findings of the study were helpful to United States and Mexico law enforcement professionals in their efforts to combat the smuggling of illicit proceeds. This was a successful initiative that not only provided information that is being used to enhance investigative efforts in regard to bulk cash smuggling, it also fosters better collaboration with our counterparts in Mexico. FinCEN continues to be supportive of such initiatives to increase vigilance in combating illicit proceeds, and facilitate law enforcement efforts to detect, disrupt, and dismantle criminal networks engaged in this kind of illegal transnational activity.

Conclusion

The Administration has made combating drug-related crime in Mexico a national priority, and as a result the Treasury Department's efforts in this regard have increased significantly over recent years through targeted financial measures, and outreach to international counterparts and our partners in the private sector. While we explore new ways in which our two countries can continue to foster collaboration, FinCEN will further build upon its excellent relationship with the UIF in support of law enforcement. Success in this regard requires the ongoing vigilance of private financial institutions and their efforts to report appropriate information to the government. By facilitating the strategic sharing of information, we can protect our financial institutions from criminal abuse while providing the government with the information it needs to track down the criminal actors. We are very encouraged by the progress we have made thus far, and we are dedicated to continuing to build on these accomplishments as we chart a course for the future. Thank you for inviting me to testify before you today. I would be happy to answer any questions you may have.

End Notes

[i]http://ondcp.gov/publications/swb_counternarcotics_strategy09/swb_counternarcotics_strategy09.pdf

[ii] http://ondcp.gov/publications/swb_implementation10/swb_ implement ation 10.pdf

[iii] http://www.ffiec.gov/bsa_aml_infobase/documents/regulations/Annunzio_Wylie.pdf

[iv] 74 FR 22129 (May 12, 2009)

[v] http://www.gpo.gov/fdsys/pkg/PLAW-111publ24/pdf/PLAW-111 publ24.pdf

[vi] http://www.egmontgroup.org/

[vii] http://www.fincen.gov/news_room/rp/files/06-2010-0238-eng-final. pdf

[viii] http://www.fincen.gov/statutes regs/guidance/html/fin-2010-a007.html

[ix] http://thomas.loc.gov/cgi-bin/query//F?c108:4:./temp/~c108zQiWCF: e11893:

[x] http://www.fincen.gov/news_room/rp/files/cross_border.html

[xi] http://www.fincen.gov/news room/rp/rulings/pdf/Implications AndBenefits OfCBFTR.pdf

In: Dirty Money
Editor: Donna P. Richards

ISBN: 978-1-61324-663-4

Chapter 7

MONEY LAUNDERING: AN ABRIDGED OVERVIEW OF 18 U.S.C. 1956 AND RELATED FEDERAL CRIMINAL LAW

Congressional Research Service

SUMMARY

Money laundering is a federal crime, most often prosecuted today under 18 U.S.C. 1956. Money laundering is commonly understood as the process of cleansing the taint from the proceeds of crime. In federal criminal law, it is more. In varying degrees under federal law, money laundering involves the flow of resources to and from several hundred other federal, state and foreign crimes. It consists of: (1) engaging in a financial transaction involving the proceeds of certain crimes in order to conceal the nature, source, or ownership of proceeds they produced; (2) transporting funds generated by certain criminal activities internationally in order to promote further criminal activities, or to conceal nature, source, or ownership of the criminal proceeds, or to evade reporting requirements; (3) engaging in a financial transaction involving the proceeds of certain crimes in order to promote further offenses; (4) engaging in a financial transaction involving criminal proceeds in order to evade taxes on the income produced by the illicit activity; (5) structuring financial transactions in order to evade reporting requirements; (6) spending more than $10,000 of the proceeds of certain criminal activities; (7) traveling in interstate or foreign commerce in order to distribute the proceeds of certain criminal activities; (8) transmitting the proceeds of criminal activity in the course of a money transmitting business; (9) smuggling unreported cash across a U.S. border, or (10) failing to comply with the Treasury Department's anti-money laundering provisions. The Supreme Court has recently indicated that the proscription in section 1956 against attempted international transportation of tainted proceeds to conceal their source, ownership, nature or ultimate location does not reach simple attempted cash smuggling without some proof of a specific concealment purpose for the smuggling. It indicated in a second case that references to the tainted "proceeds," which are the focus of section 1956, sometimes refer to the profits of a predicate offense and sometimes to its gross receipts.

18 U.S.C. 1956

Section 1956 outlaws four kinds of laundering—promotional, concealment, smurfing, and tax evasion—committed or attempted under one or more of three jurisdictional conditions— laundering involving certain financial transactions, laundering involving international transfers, and stings. More precisely, section 1956(a)(1) outlaws financial transactions involving the proceeds of other certain crimes—predicate offenses referred to as 'specified unlawful activities"—committed or attempted: (1) with the intent to promote further predicate offenses, (2) with the intent to evade taxation, (3) knowing the transaction is designed to launder the proceeds, or (4) knowing the transaction is designed to avoid anti-laundering reporting requirements. Section 1956(a)(2) outlaws the interstate or international transportation or transmission (or attempted transportation or transmission) of funds (1) with the intent to promote a predicate offense, (2) knowing that the purpose is to conceal laundering of the funds and knowing that the funds are the proceeds of a predicate offense, or (3) knowing that the purpose is to avoid reporting requirements and knowing that the funds are the proceeds of a predicate offense. Section 1956(a)(3) is a sting section. It outlaws financial transactions (or attempted transactions) that the defendant believes involve the proceeds of a predicate offense and that are intended to (1) promote a predicate offense, (2) launder the proceeds, or (3) avoid reporting requirements.

All but two of the ten section 1956 crimes are related in one or another to the commission or purported commission of at least one of a list of predicate offenses, "specified unlawful activities." The predicate offenses come in three varieties: state crimes, foreign crimes, and federal crimes. The list of state crimes is relatively short and consists of any state crime that is a RICO predicate offense, that is, any act or threat involving murder, kidnaping, gambling, arson, robbery, bribery, extortion, dealing in obscene matter, or dealing in a controlled substance or listed chemical (as defined in section 102 of the Controlled Substances Act), which is chargeable under state law and punishable by imprisonment for more than one year. The list of foreign crimes recognized as section 1956 predicate offenses is very much the same—violations of the laws of another country involving murder, kidnaping, bribery, drug trafficking and the like—but it only applies in cases involving a financial transaction occurring in whole or in part in this country. The list of federal predicate offenses is considerable longer if for no other reason than it is specific rather than generic.

Each of the ten criminal proscriptions found in section 1956 outlaws both the completed offense and the attempt to commit it. Section 1956(h) outlaws conspiracy to violate any of these proscriptions.

Consequences: Prison terms, fines, civil penalties, and confiscation may follow as a consequence of conviction of a money laundering offense. Any violation of section 1956 is punishable by imprisonment for not more than 20 years. Violations of section 1956(a)(1) and (a)(2), the financial institution and interstate or foreign transmission offenses, are punishable by a fine of no more than the greater of $500,000 or twice the value of the property involved in the offense. Sting violations are punishable by a fine of not more than the greater of $250,000 ($500,000 for an organization) or twice of amount involved in the offense. Violators of any provisions of section 1956 are subject to a civil penalty of no more than the greater of $10,000 or the value of the property involved in the offense. Forfeiture is the confiscation of property to the government as a consequence of the property's proximity to some form of criminal activity. The proceeds of a confiscation are generally shared among the law enforcement agencies that participate in the investigation and prosecution of the forfeiture. Section 1956 provides a vehicle for confiscation in two very distinct ways. First, the "proceeds" of any section 1956 predicate offense (and any property traceable to such proceeds) are subject to confiscation without the necessity of any actual violation of section 1956. Second, property "involved" in a section 1956 money laundering offense (or property traceable to such involved property) may be confiscated. The Eighth Amendment prohibits excessive fines. Fines are excessive if they are grossly disproportionate to the gravity of the offender's misconduct. While the excessive fines clause may impose limits upon the permissible extent of the confiscation for failure to comply with anti-money laundering reporting statutes, forfeitures under section 1956 are not ordinarily considered excessive because of the gravity of the offense and its predicate offenses.

18 U.S.C. 1957

Unless there is some element of promotion, concealment or evasion, section 1956 does not make simply spending or depositing tainted money a crime. Section 1957 does. It outlaws otherwise innocent transactions contaminated by the origin of the property involved in the transaction. Using most of the same definitions as section 1956, the elements of 1957 cover anyone who:

1. A. in the United States, B. in the special maritime or territorial jurisdiction of the United States, or C. outside the United States if the defendant is an American,
2. knowingly
3. A. engages or B. attempts to engage in
4. a monetary transaction
5. [in or affecting U.S. interstate or foreign commerce]
6. in criminally derived property that A. is of a greater value than $10,000 and B. is derived from specified unlawful activity.

Section 1957 also proscribes attempts to violate its provisions. Section 1956(h) outlaws conspiracy to violate section 1957. Violations of section 1957 and conspiracy to violate section 1957 are each punishable by imprisonment for not more than 10 years and/or by a fine of not more than the greater of $250,000 ($500,000 for an organization) or twice the amount involved in the transaction. Violators of section 1957 are subject to a civil penalty of no more than the greater of $10,000 or the value of the property involved in the offense. Any property involved in a violation of section 1957 or traceable to property involved in a violation of section 1957 is subject to confiscation under either civil or criminal procedures, and the applicable law is essentially the same as in the case of section 1956.

TRAVEL ACT

The money laundering provisions of sections 1956, 1957 punish transactions involving promotion, concealment, evasion, spending and depositing. The Travel Act, 18 U.S.C. 1952, punishes interstate or foreign travel (or use of the facilities of interstate or foreign commerce) conducted with the intent to distribute the proceeds of a more modest list of predicate offenses or to promote or carry on such offenses when there is an overt act in furtherance of that intent. The Travel Act is a section 1956 and 1957 predicate offense (specified unlawful activity); section 1956 and 1957 are Travel Act predicate offenses (unlawful activity); and although the money laundering predicate offense list is more extensive, several of the Travel Act predicate offenses are also money laundering predicates. The Travel Act essentially condemns three crimes each with an interstate element: the distribution of the proceeds of a predicate offense, the promotion of a predicate offense, or the commission of a violent crime in aid of a predicate offense. The first two variants bear some resemblance to the concealment and promotion offenses of section 1956 and somewhat more remotely to the deposit/spending proscriptions of section 1957. The violent crime component of the Travel Act is only coincidentally related to money laundering and consequently will be mentioned only in passing.

The courts often abbreviate their statement of the elements to encompass only whichever of the three versions is at issue:

> *Distribution*—The essential elements of a violation under section 1952(a) are: "(1) travel in interstate or foreign commerce; (2) with the specific intent to distribute the proceeds of an unlawful activity; and (3) knowing and willful commission of an act in furtherance of that intent."
>
> *Facilitation*—"The government must prove (1) interstate travel or use of an interstate facility; (2) with the intent to . . . promote . . . an unlawful activity and (3) followed by performance or attempted performance of acts in furtherance of the unlawful activity."
>
> *Violence*: "To prove a violation of the Travel Act, the government was required to establish that Ajaj: (1) used a facility of interstate or foreign commerce; (2) with intent to commit any unlawful activity (including arson. . .); and (3) thereafter performed an additional act to further the unlawful activity.

The distribution and facilitation offenses of the Travel Act, 18 U.S.C. 1952(a)(1) and 18 U.S.C. 1952(a)(3), are punishable by imprisonment for not more than five years; the crime-of-violencein-furtherance offense is punishable by imprisonment for not more than 20 years. Offenders of any of the three offenses are subject to a fine of the greater of not more than $250,000 ($500,000 for organizations) or twice the gain or loss associated with the offense. Property associated with a violation of section 1952 is not subject to confiscation solely by virtue of that fact, although the property may be confiscation by operation of the laws governing 1952 predicate offense.

31 U.S.C. 5322 - Reporting Requirements

Section 5322 penalizes willful violation of several monetary transaction reporting requirements found in Subtitle 53-II of title 31 of the United States Code and elsewhere. The section's coverage extends to violations of:

- 31 U.S.C. 5313 - financial institution reports of cash transactions involving $10,000 or more (31 C.F.R. §103.22);
- 31 U.S.C. 5314 - reports by persons in the U.S. of foreign financial agency transactions (31 C.F.R. §103.24);
- 31 U.S.C. 5316 - reports by any person taking $10,000 in cash out of the U.S. or bring it in;
- 31 U.S.C. 5318 - suspicious transaction reports by financial institutions;
- 31 U.S.C. 5325 - reports by financial institutions issuing cashier's checks in amounts of $3000 or more (31 C.F.R. §103.29);
- 31 U.S.C. 5326 - cash transaction reports by financial institutions and/or various trades or businesses pursuant to Treasury Department geographical orders (31 C.F.R. § 103.26);
- 31 U.S.C. 5331 - reports of trades and businesses other than financial institutions of cash transactions involving $10,000 or more (31 C.F.R. § 103.30);
- 12 U.S.C. 1829b - record keeping requirements of federally insured depository institutions;
- 12 U.S.C. 1953 - record keeping by uninsured banks or similar institutions.

Simple violations of section 5322 are punishable by imprisonment for not more than five years, a fine of not more the $250,000, or both. Violations committed during the commission of another federal crime or as part of a pattern of illegal activity involving more than $100,000 over the course of a year are punishable by imprisonment for not more than 10 years; a fine of not more than $500,000 (not more than $1 million for a special measures violation (31 U.S.C. 5318A) or a violation involving a breach of due diligence with respect to private banking for foreign customers or foreign shell banks (31 U.S.C. 5318(i), (j)); or both. Section 5322 is a Travel Act predicate offense and RICO predicate offense, but not a section 1956 or 1957 money laundering predicate offense. Property associated with violations of two of the sections within its coverage is subject to confiscation. Under section 5317(c) property becomes forfeitable when it is involved in, or traceable to, a violation of 31 U.S.C. 5313 (reports relating to cash transactions involving $10,000 or more) or of 31 U.S.C. 5316 (reports relating to taking $10,000 or more out of the U.S. or to bring it into the U.S.).

31 U.S.C. 5324 - Anti-Structuring

Section 5324 condemns causing the failure to file a required report, causing the submission of a false report, structuring transactions to evade a reporting requirement, or attempting to do so. Violations are punishable by imprisonment for not more than five years (not more than 10 years if committed in conjunction with another federal offense or if committed as part of a pattern of activity involving $100,000 or more) and a fine of not more than $250,000 (not more than $500,000 for organizations), with the fine maximum doubled if the offense is committed in conjunction with another federal crime or as part of a pattern of activity involving $100,000.

31 U.S.C. 5332 - Bulk Cash Smuggling

Section 5332 outlaws carrying or attempting to transport more than $10,000 in unreported, "concealed" cash across a U.S. border with the intent to evade 31 U.S.C. 5316 reporting requirements. The proscribed methods of concealment seems to envelope any method short of public display. The offense carries a prison term of not more than five years, but also calls for confiscation of the cash and related property.

18 U.S.C. 1960 - Money Transmitters

Section 1960 prohibits unlicensed money transmitting businesses and defines such businesses as (A) those that are required by state law to be licensed and are not; (B) those that fail to comply with federal regulatory provisions; and (C) those that transmit money they know is derived from, and intended to finance, criminal activity. Offenders face imprisonment for not more than five years and/or a fine of not more than $250,000 (not more than $500,000 for organizations).

Racketeer Influenced and Corrupt Organizations(RICO) - 18 U.S.C. 1961 - 1964)

All the racketeering predicate offenses listed in 18 U.S.C. 1961(1) are by definition money laundering predicate offenses under sections 1956 and 1957. RICO makes it a federal crime for any person to:

1. conduct or participate, directly or indirectly, in the conduct of
2. the affairs of an enterprise
3. engaged in or the activities of which affect, interstate or foreign commerce
4. A. through the collection of an unlawful debt, or
B. through a pattern of racketeering activity (predicate offenses).

RICO violations are punishable by imprisonment for not more than 20 years (not more than life imprisonment if any of the applicable predicate offenses carries a life sentence). Offenders also face fines of up to $250,000 (up to $500,000 for organizations) as well as the confiscation of any property associated with the offense. They may also be liable to their victims for triple damages, and subject to the equitable remedies, at least the behest of the government.

The Supreme Court has recently held that the proscription in section 1956 against attempted international transportation of tainted proceeds for the purpose of concealing the ownership, source, nature of ultimate location is limited to instances where concealment is a purpose rather than an attribute of the transportation (simple smuggling is not proscribed as such), *United States v. Cuellar*, 128 S.Ct. 1994 (2008). In a second case, the Court indicated that for purposes of section 1956 the "proceeds" of a predicate offense refers to gross receipts rather than profits realized from the offense, unless the nature of the predicate offense and the penalty it carries renders such a result "perverse," *United States v. Santos*, 128 S.Ct. 2020 (2008).

CHAPTER SOURCES

Chapter 1 – This is an edited, reformatted and augmented version of United States Government Accountability Office Report GAO-11-73, dated October 2010.

Chapter 2 – This is an edited, reformatted and augmented version of remarks delivered as testimony given before the Senate Caucus on International Narcotics Control regarding a Hearing on Money Laundering and Bulk Cash Smuggling Across the Southwest Border on March 9, 2011. Dianne Feinstein is a U.S. Senator.

Chapter 3 – This is an edited, reformatted and augmented version of United States Government Accountability Office Report GAO-11-407T, dated March 9, 2011.

Chapter 4 – This is an edited, reformatted and augmented version of remarks delivered as testimony given before the Senate Caucus on International Narcotics Control regarding a Hearing on Money Laundering and Bulk Cash Smuggling Across the Southwest Border on March 9, 2011. Alan Bersin is Commissioner of U.S. Customs and Border Protection in the Department of Homeland Security.

Chapter 5 – This is an edited, reformatted and augmented version of remarks delivered as testimony given before the Senate Caucus on International Narcotics Control regarding a Hearing on Money Laundering and Bulk Cash Smuggling Across the Southwest Border on March 9, 2011. Kumar C. Kibble is Deputy Director of U.S. Immigration and Customs Enforcement in the Department of Homeland Security.

Chapter 6 – This is an edited, reformatted and augmented version of remarks delivered as testimony given before the Senate Caucus on International

Narcotics Control regarding a Hearing on Money Laundering and Bulk Cash Smuggling Across the Southwest Border on March 9, 2011. Jamal El-Hindi is Associate Director for Regulatory Policy and Programs in the Financial Crimes Enforcement Network in the U.S. Department of the Treasury.

Chapter 7 – This is an edited, reformatted and augmented version of Congressional Research Service Report RS22401, dated July 18, 2008.

INDEX

#

A

B

C

D

E

F

I

J

L

M

N

O

P

R

S

T

U

V

W